C000116707

Channelled from Spirit
by Janet Neville
Written by Steve Bridger

Being
Spirit

You are spirit in human form

Copyright © 2019 Janet Neville and Steve Bridger

The moral right of the author has been asserted.

Apart from any fair dealing for the purposes of research or private study,
or criticism or review, as permitted under the Copyright, Designs and Patents
Act 1988, this publication may only be reproduced, stored or transmitted, in
any form or by any means, with the prior permission in writing of the
publishers, or in the case of reprographic reproduction in accordance with
the terms of licences issued by the Copyright Licensing Agency. Enquiries
concerning reproduction outside those terms should be sent to the publishers.

Matador
9 Priory Business Park,
Wistow Road, Kibworth Beauchamp,
Leicestershire. LE8 0RX
Tel: 0116 279 2299
Email: books@troubador.co.uk
Web: www.troubador.co.uk/matador
Twitter: @matadorbooks

ISBN 978 1789017 830

British Library Cataloguing in Publication Data.
A catalogue record for this book is available from the British Library.

Printed and bound in Great Britain by 4edge Limited
Typeset in 12pt Garamond by Troubador Publishing Ltd, Leicester, UK

Matador is an imprint of Troubador Publishing Ltd

We would like to dedicate this book to:
Our Guides in Spirit

Mary & Bill Butlin,
Peter & Edna Lucy Bridger,
Jean Mackenzie

In loving memory of

Patsy Wood

Heartfelt thanks to:

Allan Watt
Bernadete May
Maria Morris
Jack & Jackie McCaugherty
Lesley Hamilton
Liz Alpe
Karen Pyle
Ann Richardson
Lily Jenkins
Nigel Peace

Reactions to Being Spirit

Dean Cox

"When it comes to spiritualism I am a total blank page, I am totally neutral; I do not believe or dis-believe. I think from that point of view the book goes over my head, but on almost every page I read beautiful sentiments which can't be a bad thing. It seems that the messages from the spirits are about Love & Peace and that makes it compelling reading."

Katherine Bolton

"I have been lucky enough to sit in many different circles in many countries and as a fellow psychic I am very often asked about what happens and what goes on. Being Spirit enables the newcomer as well as the more experienced to understand what happens. It is written in a very easy to read style which never comes across as being condescending. I have already recommended this book to several friends and also to my friends in my circle. Well done Janet and Steve for a brilliant book. I look forward to your next one."

Santosh Sagoo

"Upon receiving my copy I started to read my book straight away – Wow! It's magical. So far what I've read make sense. It's clear and I understand the words and messages. I like the writing style and the flow (and font size). I'm enjoying the read and the penny is dropping as I'm beginning to understand things more."

Lucy Blanc

"I'm halfway through reading your book. When I started to read it I planned to earmark pages of great interest. I have just looked and most all the pages are earmarked already! Thoughts on reaching you higher self should be a daily mantra for all. I have some questions, although the book has done a fantastic job in explaining the how's and why's of spirit. I have picked up a fair bit of understanding of how spirit works but the book covers topics that seamlessly piece it all together in a way it all makes sense."

Tom Hollamby

"Being Spirit" The very title is intriguing. It is a thoughtful and often inspiring journey to the inner nature of Mankind. This is a serious search into the dynamics of peace and love. The authors' often quote not only personal but universal, historical and temporal sources for their assertions. Following their own tenets of being guided by gentle, persuasive and convincing arguments, they reach through space and time to support their theses. This is a sensitive and often mind provoking read into the realms of life and spirituality."

Wendy Harvey

"I have just finished your book on spirit. My thoughts are this book will really help people who do feel alone. It opens your mind to the spirit world and makes it very easy to understand. I would be happy to recommend this book to anybody so they can feel and fall in love with spirit. Please keep up the good work I'm looking forward to the next book."

Welcome Friend

You are a spiritual being. A spirit in human form.
Being spirit is your eternal state.

This book is an invitation to explore and embrace your own
spirituality.

Being Spirit was instigated by eight Native American
spirit guides. Their guidance is the bedrock of this book.
They will speak to you in their own words. The messages
in Being Spirit were channelled from spirit by Janet Neville.
This is spirit's description of the book in two sentences:

*The book will be like a magical pathway where it will dawn upon
many that they are not alone in your world. It is not a story
about the realms of spirit but a story of how one can connect,
work, and be at one with spirit while still on your earth.*

Chapter by chapter will unfold with unchanged messages
direct from spirit. This extract explains how this book came
about:

The whole purpose of this venture is one that has been in discussion for a long time. There are many written words about our world. People choose to write on various subjects which are close to their hearts. There have been many written words on angels. There are numerous writings on how angels help and protect and can transcend from spirit to earth in the wake of atrocities to help lessen the trauma from the terrors which occur on your earth.

There are many written words about the realms of spirit; how in each realm there are spheres and planes, how a spirit has to work towards reaching each level, how a spirit does not stop learning.

A spirit is always learning and evolving towards the divine light.

It is all there on many written pages.

This was all in a discussion until the spirit named Blue Flame spoke out and mentioned that although every possible avenue had been placed on parchment, there was something missing, which were pages filled with the written words in simplistic terms. Where a person who is interested in our world would be able to gain a glimpse into how our world is shaped.

Here's a message from Five Arrows who is a member of the group of eight guides that inspired this book:

My friend, in our world we want everyone to know the truth that not only is life eternal, but we are there to help, protect and guide. We can help relieve the pressure from your hectic lives. We can help relieve stress and disharmony.

We want people to give a thought of what is beyond your living life; and have a small amount of belief and trust that we will be there in times of stress and hardships. We want no rewards or praise we just want to help those who need it. We want you to know there is a gentle force that cares and that the most important work of our world is to spread the love that is within you. Be sure that you will be offered the peace and enlightenment that will help you through all of life's trials.

Spirit guides once lived on earth. Falling in love, raising families, joy and heartbreak, triumphs and disappointments, falling ill and getting well, were the tapestry of their existence just like ours. They would have loved and lost their loved ones just like us. Think of them as real people who lived their lives on earth and that they are our lifelong friends and guides:

We are your friends. We come with the kind of friendship that blends into the love that only spirit can give. Love is given in its purest form. Once given we do not take it back. It's our wish not only to help people with their development and to understand our world, but to be able to connect in a way you would do with a friend in your physical world.

To be a friend with someone on the earth is to be able to relax in their company and not to be afraid to place your own opinions in the conversations for fear of being rebuked. Friendship is to recognise when one or the other is feeling down and needs a helping hand; whether it is given with discretion or verbally. True friendship is where each other can blend together therefore overcoming any misunderstandings that may arise, to be able to voice one's own mind and opinion, laugh together and cry together, in other words to be totally natural.

The aim for this book is to engage and inform. It is for anyone seeking to explore their own spirituality. We'd like to stress that what you're about to read is not critical of any beliefs of faith you may already hold. If you have no beliefs, this book may be an agent of change.

Janet Neville is a spiritual medium who acts as the link between our world and the world of spirit. She channelled messages using the spoken or written word on different subjects, at different times, over months of contact. My role as writer was to create the narrative content. Spirit guided, shaped and inspired the words you're about to read. One point to clarify is that the messages received throughout the book by Janet are 'addressed' as if they are personal letters to me as the writer to pass on to you.

Contents

One

Living Spirit

How it began: Wednesday 14th December 2016

I arrived late. Janet was in full flow. A non-stop three way conversation was taking place. The congregation were silent, straining to hear, not wanting to miss a single word. Only two people were visibly engaged. Janet in a flame red dress was instantaneously listening, laughing and talking to a girl in the second row. I realised that a millisecond pause punctuated Janet's message, as if someone off-stage was feeding her information, like an actor forgetting their lines and getting a prompt. This was exactly what was happening, except that the prompt was coming from another world.

Janet must have spoken to at least five more people that night. I lost count. Giving proof and supplying information was the first thing she did. It was personal, direct confirmation that was accepted by each person that mothers, fathers, sisters, brothers, wives, husbands, sons, daughters and friends were clearly identified and wanted to communicate from spirit and pass on their undying love.

They may not be in this world, but they were very much alive in the next.

Janet stepped down from the platform and was showered with thanks. We were in the spiritual church in Kingston-Upon-Thames in Surrey, England, the same church where Sir Arthur Conan Doyle, creator of Sherlock Holmes, laid the foundation stone on the 27th April 1927. Over ninety years ago.

Bernadete, Janet's friend and fellow spiritual medium made the introductions over a cup of tea:

Janet, this is Steve, he's a writer.
Janet paused, thought, smiled and spoke.
They said you would come. They said this would be the beginning.

The tea went cold, time slipped past unnoticed. Our meeting was no accident. We knew there was a need to talk about spirit using simple language that anyone could understand.

We wanted to explain spirit in a way that would be accepted in hearts and minds by as many people as possible.

The principal obligation of spiritual mediumship is to provide evidence. This book goes one step further. Being Spirit has been written with the direct participation of spirit guides. They have instigated this project to provide proof of their existence and to share knowledge.

The guides are eight Native American Indians. They describe themselves as the Group, you'll meet them soon. Janet and I are their earth-based link. Janet channels messages transmitted from spirit by thought energy in one of two ways. One results in her receiving, let's call them letters from Heaven, where she writes the messages onto her tablet then sends them to me to weave into the flow of the book. The second method is where Janet enters into a state of consciousness described as channelling or direct voice, where she speaks the words of spirit. These are recorded then added to the text. We'll say more about channelling later. All that we are about to share has been communicated by spirit guides to give to you.

The content of Being Spirit is intended as a starting point, a stimulus to learning more about spirit and their world. Spirit will always be at the core of your being. That's what being spirit is all about. It is the invisible part of you that continues to evolve with every new experience. Perhaps a loved one has recently passed and grief is consuming you. Could it be that you're looking for proof that they are safe in spirit? It may be that you've sensed spirit in your life and want to understand more. It could be that you're starting to question beliefs that have been passed down to you since childhood and you're no longer prepared to accept just because it was expected of you. Perhaps you are thirsting for spiritual knowledge in your own right. There is no conflict with conventional religious thought. It is a question of becoming more spiritually aware yourself.

What you are about to read has been guided by spirit. It is for you alone. The messages are to help you understand the reality of another world, a world driven by the power of thought, a world of peace and love. These messages have been written to make you aware of the divine energy you have within you. These communications are an awakening for you to realise that being spirit is your natural and eternal state. Spirit wanted to explain:

The purpose of communication from our world to yours is to prove that life is eternal. Your spirit is impossible to extinguish, it will live forever in thought and energy. The main purpose is to prove to the friends and loved ones of the deceased that while they have left their earthly body, they are very much alive in spirit and energy.

It gives great joy and comfort for any spirit to be able to make this communication back to the earth. It's sent with an abundance of love and happiness. We in our world understand that it can be a very emotional experience for a person on the earth to receive a message from beyond the earth's boundaries. If the message is delivered with pure love and clarity then the recipient will experience a warm glow and the feeling of calm and peace that their loved one is happy, safe and secure. This will enable that person to grieve in a way that will help them come to terms with their loss.

Spirit in Human Form

'I'm a spiritual person.' People often say this but it's not always clear what they mean. It may be the love of nature or a belief in some higher power or an attempt to deflect questions about religion. They are right. They are spirit in human form. Each one of us is unique with a character that embodies our own indefinable personality that's evident to the world. We are all human spirits. Janet's spirit guide gave her this view of the spiritual process that affects us all:

Before you were born you were pure energy in the world of spirit. This purity of spirit is with you at conception in the material world. Simultaneously your soul, the beating heart of your human emotions, joins your life from that moment onward. Spirit and soul become one. When your time on earth is over you return to spirit shaped by the physical life you have led.

When your spirit returns from earth it goes through a cleansing cycle. It's as if you're presented by a book of your life from beginning to end. You will be faced with the actions you took, the decisions you made, how you treated others, and your behaviour towards people, animals and the environment. At the same time the positive developments are noted too. The care and consideration you're shown along with the successes you've enjoyed and progress you've made are recognised. This cleansing will be a process of atonement that must be completed before your spirit can rise higher.

All that's been said so far, and all that's about to be said, reinforces one central belief. It is that we are living in two parallel worlds at the same time, one physical one spiritual. We exist in both side by side. We come from spirit and will return to spirit. This is our existence, two strands of intertwined life. Our time on earth in a physical state provides our spirit with the experience of feeling joy, pleasure, love, hate, jealousy, pain and anguish, all the emotions. For our spirit it is a time of challenge, development and growth.

Accepting we are spiritual beings changes our entire outlook on life. The material world and our experiences within it, good and bad, success or failure are stepping stones on our pathway. Evidence from spirit from loved ones who have passed shows us there isn't a forbidding black hole at the end of life but an open door to experience a new life.

Spirit within Us

Human spirit is an unquantifiable factor in our lives. It is the source of astounding energy. We watch in awe as people survive unbelievable traumas. They tap into hidden strengths to amaze us with their resilience. This is part of the human spirit we can see. It is evidence of the divine energy within us that we witness with our own eyes.

How can we explain this? Forgive this over-simplification of this interaction between mind and brain. For our purposes we will say they are two interlinked elements. One relates to the brain and the physical functions of the body. The other is the mind, the thought centre of emotions, creativity, memories, intuition, of our consciousness and of our conscience.

We know that doctors and scientists can record and convert energy transmitted by the brain into electrical pulses. You only have to watch hospital programmes on television to see the monitors recording the body's vital signs bleeping in the background. Energy is also generated by the mind causing vibrations created by thought. Instead of electrical pulses we have thought pulses that stem from the mind.

It is this spiritual energy generated by thought from the mind that is human spirit. It is human spirit that opens and powers the channels of communication with the spirit world. This message is direct from spirit and explains how they work with human spirit and reveals that they send ideas disguised as your own intuition.

This is what they say:

It is by thought that spirit is able to connect with the human spirit. Thought processes play an important part with the communication from our world to yours, which is how we work. From our part it is but a simple process to deliver the message through the invisible link. To allow the human spirit to define the information that has been relayed to them is difficult. We understand that in the mind there are many other thoughts from your material life swirling around. Making it difficult to define as to whether it is coming from spirit or yourself.

We do work in another way which is intuition. This is your gut instinct. This way of working is most probably the commonest way in which spirit works but it is very rarely recognised as spirit communication. It gets ignored time and time again. It's a common idea among people wishing to connect with our world that a booming voice that will sound within earshot and they'll see a spirit suddenly appear. You know my friend that is not how it works.

With intuition we drop the seed of thought into a person's mind. This seed then transforms into what you on your earth would describe as gut instinct. It can then become like a gnawing sensation which is us trying to guide you onto the pathway to solve the problem which has been causing distress, or just to guide you to the correct solution of which you seek.

Most times this input is ignored. Spirit works with everyone on your earth and not only those who wish our input and that is where the difficulty can occur, especially for those of you who consciously work with Spirit. This can be frustrating in our world for the simple reason we are trying to guide that person onto the right decision in their mind. If they ignore our signal then it can become frustrating not only for them but for us, especially when we witness that person walking along the wrong path. We in our group of guides feel *it would be of importance for this to be made clear to the reader.*

Soul Deep

Often in conventional religion, the word soul has an interchangeable meaning with the word spirit to signify a person's total spirituality. She's very soulful. He's very spiritual. In addition to the core group of eight guides, Janet has her own circle of guides in the spirit world led by her main guide Running Water a Navaho Indian. This spirit group has a number of visiting guides; Wang Chang is one of them. He is a highly evolved Chinese teaching guide and wished to add this piece:

> *Spirit is an everlasting state of being. The soul is the reflection of human experience while on earth. Your soul is your emotions. Your spirit is your personality, put the two together they become one. Your personality is what drives you, your character, the introvert you or the extrovert you. Your emotions are the deep inner you. It's the real you where you feel hurt, love, anger, hate. Combining the two isn't always easy. Sometimes it's difficult for people to express their feelings; sometimes people are all too open, sometimes emotions can be like a locked-up cupboard.*

All the emotional and physical actions and reactions are logged as perfect memories inside the soul. Every happening during your lifetime is recorded in your mind to capture your experience on earth. These memories are entered into your spiritual book of life.

Your soul is a barometer of the depth of caring and feeling and your emotional sensitivity. Being soulful is an outward expression of your character and love for others. As we grow from childhood and get immersed in the material world it is easy to think that struggling for gain is the name of the game. Success has a different meaning for each of us. For many people material wealth is everything, for others overcoming health issues could be a truly satisfying achievement. Whatever the situation never lose sight of your soul.

Your Higher Self

The oneness of soul and spirit at the beginning of life created your higher self. Throughout your life you'll experience occasions when your higher self makes itself known to you.

This could be with flashes of inspiration, or with feelings of undiluted joy with loved ones, of euphoria. Recapture instances like those in your mind. Remember the elation you felt? That's spirit giving you sensations of the divine, a glimpse of being your higher self.

Here are thoughts on reaching your best self, suggested by our invisible friends in spirit:

1. Forgive yourself. Apologise for acts of the past. You don't get to the age you are without acting selfishly or nastily. Notice that I stressed the past, because with forgiveness you're already starting to move forward.
2. Say sorry and ask forgiveness from all those people you've hurt in the past. If you remember their names, speak them out loud as you bring them to mind.

3. Turn your attention to hang-ups and ideas that have held you back. Jettison negative and limiting beliefs. You know in your heart that you are better than that.

4. Try to do at least one random act of kindness a day. Not just the easy ones but ones that require a little effort. Show care and consideration; take action to help others.

5. Think cheerful thoughts and be more positive in everything you do. You'll surprise yourself. Blow away the thunderclouds that used to hover over your head. Smile you are alive.

6. Live in the now. Don't waste time making plans for the future while the present goes begging. The past has gone; the future hasn't happened so relish the sights, sounds, smells and situations that surround you as you take your next breath. Create the memories you'll soon be looking back on. Many of us are emotional casualties of the past. Here's a phrase for not being caught like a frozen statue and wasting your life by thinking about tomorrows that will never come: "Today is the tomorrow you worried about yesterday."

7. Understand that to develop and grow into your higher self you need to value and care for the animal kingdom and all living things. Animals are spirit beings too. Realise that you are a guardian of this world. Realise that by protecting all living things on earth and protecting the oceans and marine life you are part of the spirit workforce.

8. Meditate and take time out for yourself. Pause the hustle and bustle, cut the static from your daily grind and concentrate upon yourself. Meditation is a great way to relax and destress your mind and body. It is also a prime pathway for connecting with spirit.

9. The earth plane is at one with the universe. The universe is one with the spirit world. Your aim is to become one with your higher self. This will take time but you could start edging towards it today. It is the divine light at the end of the tunnel.

If you're someone who likes to be more specific you could join campaigns against global warming, child poverty, famine and clean water in Africa, banning plastic bags and microbeads being thrown into our oceans. This news report is one example: a distressed whale that was put down after repeatedly becoming stranded off the Norway coast. The whale had 30 plastic bags wedged inside its stomach.

(Source: University of Bergen)

A last word on the 'F' Word

The past can paralyze. Harm that has been done to you or that you have done can imprison you in a stagnant state of 'now'. You may be imprisoned by past acts and events that have brought feelings of shame, guilt and remorse. The only way to break the chains is to forgive. No one said it would be easy.

Forgiveness works both ways. Forgiving those who have damaged you frees you to move forward. To continue the analogy, this is your get out of jail card. Hating others channels positivity in the wrong direction. Negative energy benefits nobody and keeps you locked in yesterday. If the person who has hurt you has passed into the afterlife, your forgiveness will allow them to atone and move forward but only after they have shown remorse and apologised to you.

Forgiving yourself is often the hardest thing to do. Feeling anguish over past deeds is a relentless self-inflicted punishment. To use a religious term you would be in a never ending purgatory of pain. No good will come of this. An effective form of repentance is to decide from today onwards to be the person you were born to be with acts of kindness wherever and whenever you can. Crucially, you will move forward leaving bitterness behind. Face down your past and live in the present.

This is a message from the group of guides on forgiveness:

When a spirit chooses the right to a life the choice is given to them as to which pathway they would like to experience. No spirit chooses to be evil, no spirit chooses to kill or maim innocent people. No spirit chooses to hurt those who they are to love. Those choices are made within the human mind when they start their life's journey. It's an accumulation of many of life's rituals or mental illness that can interfere with the way their minds are working. The choice of right and wrong are within everyone to understand. They are within your emotions. They are there to help guide you along the way.

The majority of people living within your earth abide by these rules. It's common for people to stray a little away from these rules. Every person on earth at one time in their lives have been guilty of causing distress or slight harm to another, but a stronger emotion guilt is there to help that person understand their actions and hopefully make amends to the injured party. They have to learn within themselves that you have to earn forgiveness. If you can't forgive and love others, how can you expect to be forgiven and loved?

Coming next:

We opened the book with an example of spiritual mediumship and began the process of increasing your awareness of spirit in your daily life. In the next chapter we'll explain the difference between people who have psychic abilities and those who have additional training to follow their vocation to become a spiritual medium.

Two

Spiritual Mediums
Messengers of Evidence

Rain Cloud provided this wonderful introduction to spiritual mediums and the way awareness of mediumship has developed over the years:

> *For centuries people have had communication from our world, spirits have channelled much information to the energies of people on the earth. In years gone by these people would have had to keep our prophecies secret from others. In certain parts of the globe our world would have been taboo, it would have been forbidden to talk of such matters. Although many of the scribes and prophets of years long gone had been used as channels for spirit and this would have been recognised within those who had been chosen. They would have accepted the fact that they had a special gift bestowed upon them and would have embraced the opportunity to be able to spread their prophecies and knowledge to whoever*

would listen. My friend many did listen and believe. There were also the ones who would shy away from these people in disbelief and fear. However, over the centuries our word has always managed to filter through to many minds helping and guiding those who needed a nudge in the right direction.

When it became apparent that a living person could make communication from a spirit our world then suddenly became known and accepted, albeit the numbers of believers were minimal. Over time we have worked hard with filtering our thoughts and energies onto the minds of many in order for them to be able to accept our world. This takes time and patience my friend of which we have plenty we are in no rush. It's you on your earth who feel they have to rush along doing everything all in one day.

Throughout the years people have been made to feel afraid when the subject of our world has been broached. Many religions have made our world a taboo subject. This is through fear of the unknown and a lopsided love of their own beliefs. Many cannot find it in themselves to widen the horizon of their minds to try and understand what is in front of them. They are aware we are there but choose to dismiss us with a negative mind.

In these more modern times on your earth we are fully aware that we have now become more accepted and it is no longer a criminal act to promote our world to spread the love of which we are passionate about. God spreads love wherever it can be touched and felt it's a common factor that ever since time began and man walked upon the earth. God has always found a way to touch the soul of man with his golden hand. It is the infinite and divine light made up of the purest spirit.

We can now work with more ease with our mediums. Everyone on your earth has the potential to work alongside spirit. We are there with every living soul each and every day of your lives. The numbers of lights we are attracted to are fewer than we would like. We would be jubilant if every living soul on earth accepted our presence. Alas my friend, this will never be. We will have to be content with the numbers that are devoted to us which we find are increasing in numbers in a steady stream.

When our messengers on the earth perform public services within the churches and halls it is like a blessing for us each time they serve. It's a gift from them to us. We rejoice in the fact that they are working endlessly to help spread the existence of our world with unconditional love. Every person who works in any way for spirit are treated as equals. We do not feel any one person is more important than the next, whether they make the tea or stand upon the platform you are all just as important to us.

Promoting our world need not be serious. We rejoice each time a soul comes back to the homeland it is a happy time for us all. It gives us the greatest pleasure when we can prove through our mediums that a loved one is still very much alive albeit in energy and thought. Witnessing that moment when a loved one on the earth is filled with emotion knowing that their departed is happy and much loved in our world fills us with joy and warmth. We are not there to entertain as a fairground amusement we are there to prove that life is eternal.

My friend there is also this form of communication where we channel our thoughts through the minds of mediums many are used for this purpose. There have been many written words set out in verse. There have been poems, chapters and pages on all manner of subjects. Each word channelled from spirit is a gift from us to you. My friend the gift is reversed when these words are read by you on your earth. It then becomes a gift from you to us. We rejoice in the fact that our world has been very much implanted onto the minds of many so that you can learn from our knowledge, and receive the love and shine within the light that surrounds you.

It is a joy for all spirits to communicate in whatever form is accessible. My friend it is a joy for me to be able to communicate to you in this way, and there will be many more such communications from myself. Your respected friend Rain Cloud.

Janet continues the theme of mediumship by explaining more about her calling:

It's easy for people to get confused between psychic mediums and spiritual mediums. Psychic mediums use their psychic talents to read auras to gain knowledge about a person. Psychics are sometimes referred to as fortune tellers as they focus on predicting current or future events. Psychics rely on their sense of intuition to gather information. They read people's auras using their E.S.P (Extra Sensory Perception) skills. Spiritual mediums are not fortune tellers. They don't use their psychic skills to predict the future.

Spiritual mediums receive information direct from the spirit world by working with their guides. Messages they receive give comfort and encouragement to people who may have recently lost a loved one. It may be to confirm that their pain and suffering is over, to provide advice on a private or family matter. This is personal proof that life continues in an everlasting state. An essential part of any message is to share love. Many spiritual mediums finish a message with the words: 'I'll leave their love with you.' Spiritual mediums will never divulge really personal details in an open service. Delicate personal messages will be delivered during a private session.

Spirit says more about the gift of communication:

The gift for communication to spirit is within you all. It is there rooted deep within the inner self waiting to come to the fore. It is there for many reasons and purposes. To help give and receive comfort, to let you know that you are not alone in a world where there is much sorrow and grief, to give and gain wisdom, courage, strength and humility. These are given to all who choose to accept them with the love and grace of which they are delivered. There is also the greatest gift of all which is the love that is transmitted from our world to yours. Through all the sadness that happens in your world there are volumes of love showering your earth to help those who are suffering from the loss of a loved one, from pain within themselves, from the atrocities that mankind create towards their fellow man or for the damage which is being caused to your precious earth through thoughtless minds.

That message reinforces the relationship between mankind and spirit. On an individual spiritual level it is an intensely simple, direct, private and unbreakable bond. It's not a group thing like being one follower amongst many of a religion. It's accepting that you and spirit are one and the same. That's true, even though right now, you are spiritually work-in-progress.

When you were little, did you have an imaginary friend to play with? Did you give them a name and feel happy and safe when they were around? This was your psychic radar working. We are all born with psychic potential with spirit inside. Many leave this element lying dormant and ignored. Your intuition is a daily expression of psychic activity. Your intuition will sense something over and above the five senses of touch, smell, hearing, taste and sight.

Some people experience this sixth sense from a very early age with others it slowly becomes apparent over time. With many it remains undiscovered throughout all their time on earth. It is the added psychic awareness that complements the five senses. A psychic may enjoy a combination of ESP talents. They are known by the prefix 'Clair' which is the French word for 'clear' here are the ones you may have heard but perhaps are not sure what they stand for:

Clairvoyance: Clear seeing is when images are visualised in the mind. It can be a vision from the past, present or sometimes in dreams or when tuned into spirit. It may feature people, places or symbols.

Clairsentient: Clear feeling is linked to sense of touch or feeling. It's when you're sensitive to intuitive sensations from the mind. This may be linked to feelings about a person or animal.

Clairaudience: Clear hearing from the mind, not through your ears. You hear words, sound or music in your head from spirit and not out loud.

Claircognisance: Clear knowing, is having a premonition or insight into something that is about to happen without any logical explanation.

Auras

The human body emits an aura. It's an electro-magnetic field. In your mind's eye imagine it like the glow of vibrational energy. Auras have a colour that reflects your personality. At times auras change colour to suit a particular emotional and mental state, joyful or sad, healthy or ill. Our auras emit energy from which the psychic can interpret a person's health and mental state. By physical contact, holding hands for example, physics can draw more information about the person at a particular moment in time. They can make predictions about romance, health and money matters that relate to their current situation. You've probably heard people say things like he/she has such an amazing aura around him/her meaning they have charisma, a certain attractive style or a strong physical presence. This message from source is on the theme of auras:

> Spirit see only lights, we do not see things in matter form. We only tune into the living energies. Any being with a beating heart that lives and breathes is what spirit recognises. It is the aura, the energy field around a living form that attracts spirit. There can be colours around the aura which tell of the person's situation in that particular time. Some can be green tinged with blue, some can be red of all different shades, different mauves tinged with blue, some can be white and sparkling, some dull and cloudy, some can have the colours of the rainbow layer upon layer. All these colours can give an experienced medium an indication of how that person is coping with an emotional trauma, health issues, or problems involving their material world or general wellbeing.

Spiritual Mediumship: Our minds are where the power lies.

Spiritual mediums differ from psychics as they receive their information from the spirit world, from their personal guide and other communicating spirits. Messages confirm that loved ones are watching, caring and helping from the other side of life. Some messages can be extremely mundane but they're still solid evidence of life after leaving. 'Check some important paperwork, it's time you changed your car, you need to slow down'. These are everyday examples from friends and loved ones who have passed into spirit. They may sound ordinary but they will have real significance to the persons receiving the message.

Spiritual mediums use the energy of mind and thought to connect with their spirit guides. Once the link has been established there are several forms of psychic activity to stream messages. Clairvoyance is commonly demonstrated in spiritual churches. These provide evidence of continuing life in spirit after the physical body dies. The medium sees an image in their minds eye of the person in spirit. The departed spirit is described so they can be recognised and a relevant message is often shared with someone on earth.

Janet describes her experience:

This is what it's like for me to deliver clairvoyant messages to members of the congregation during a church service. The hymn singing really lifts the energy. Once everyone has sat down and the chairperson hands the service over to me then it feels like crystal clear energy surrounds me. I can sense it around my ears and throat. It's as if I've stepped slightly aside as I start to feel their energy arrive. The information begins to flow from my spirit guide. Our energies are working as one in complete harmony. My guide is contacted by the guide of the deceased person who wishes to communicate with love ones on earth. My guide acts as the go-between. He's in charge and manages the interaction. He is there to filter through the messages to make sure they stick to the three golden rules of never to give bad news, never to give anyone's business away and never embarrass anyone. Once my guide approves the messages he stands back, and allows the communication to begin. Then the energy of the communicating spirit comes very close to my energies. That is when I'm directed to the friend or relative sitting in the congregation. I can tell exactly what the person in spirit was like when they were on the earth. They give me information about themselves. This is very fine tuning. We get the full personality of them for example, if they swore, laughed a lot, were moody or not a nice person. They can't hide anything; they're not allowed to. After the spirit is recognised then a message is given to provide evidence of life after passing.

How do I know who to go to? Spirit indicates where the person is sitting. It's automatic, without thinking my arm shoots out. I'm guided by a light above their head that picks them out. It is very rare that we go to the wrong person and if I do, I know immediately. Obviously there are times when the message or communicator cannot be recognised, that can be down to many things. The sitter can be negative and only wants a certain piece of evidence or to hear from a particular person to come through. As a medium, I realise it can at times be hard to understand or recognise the evidence I'm giving as it's coming so quickly. Some people need to think and when you're on the platform we only have a short time during the service and don't have time to let them digest all the evidence, because by waiting for a response the energy I'm feeling would plummet. When I get on a roll it's hard to stop me.

You can get a queue of spirits wanting to come through all at the same time. With the proper training between me and the guide it's very easy for me to separate them. This is all done within seconds. It's all down to trusting and harmony between them and me. Most mediums don't know who they are going to until they are directed by their own guide. Sometimes a medium doesn't get a clear link and has to describe the person in spirit in the hope they'll be recognised. When a medium connects with a friend or relative from the spirit world, the first task is to gain proof of the departed spirits identity.

The second is to pass on a message of personal significance. Usually this begins by describing what the departed spirit looks like: gender, height, body shape, what they're wearing, hair colour, general aspects that will help recognition. There is no set order, the description builds with details from spirit. It helps when I mention the family or friend relationship on the mother or father's side of the family. If it's a family member it usually goes back to grandparent. Any further back the sitter may have trouble remembering the departed spirit. In many cases the spirit will describe what illness they suffered at the time of their passing or mention any dramatic circumstances of their departure, as long as they are not too upsetting for the person and of course, for the congregation to listen to.

Often the visiting spirit will give other clues to their identity by drawing attention to a photo in a family album or a treasured possession or item of jewellery or family pet. Recently a grandmother told how she used to take her granddaughter out to feed the ducks when she was a little girl. Recalling memories is a proven way of confirming relationships. Once the identity of the departed spirit has been established there would normally be a message. This maybe something as simple as sending their love and letting people know they are around them and caring for them. It maybe that they have come through because they are worried about their health or career or family circumstances. The messages are almost always of encouragement, love and hope that have particular significance.

You could expect these sessions to be serious and gloomy. You'll be surprised how much laughter there is. I like to reflect the personality of the spirit guest. When someone passes into spirit they stay the same as you remember them. If they were happy, cheeky, naughty, tricky, if they were a joker on earth, they remain the same in the spirit world. Recently I had to moderate the language as the spirit was getting a little coarse and punctuated his message with swear words. The spirit's relatives were crying with laughter as it captured him perfectly. He was a lovable rogue.

Over the years I have given many readings to people who have been guided my way by my invisible friends. It is they who invite people along to witness the communication from them to us. There have been a few occasions when I or someone else has invited a person or persons but if they're not meant to have that experience then something will block their way from joining us for example, their car will break down or be delayed by traffic jams. Each message is special to that individual. Some will ask what seems to me to be a trivial question but it is important to them. Every time there has been a meeting between the two worlds there have been many tears shed of relief and joy from the knowledge that the person they needed to hear from is happy and safe now that they are back home in spirit. They take comfort in their lives from this most personal of all proof that life does go on and at some point they will be reunited.

Being a medium is not a get-rich-quick option. It's a way of life. The word vocation is accurate as our gifts are used to help others. Being a messenger of spirit is selfless. By serving, you are performing the most wonderful act of sharing love and light. Spiritual mediums are ambassadors of the divine light. It can take years before someone training to become a medium is sufficiently prepared to undertake that role. As you would expect a medium has to be extremely sensitive and understanding. People who've recently lost a loved one would be overwrought with emotion and need a gentle touch. Developing this sensitivity takes time and practice. Trainee mediums should not give readings before they have hours of practice and the guidance of experienced mentors. In my case, I had no inkling of any psychic ability. My realisation came out of the blue. Spirit must have decided it was my time. Before they made their presence felt, all I knew was that there was something I couldn't put my finger on. It was a hankering after something but I did not know what that was. But they did:

There are many signs a person can experience when spirit decides it is someone's time to step on their chosen path. Many feel an unsettling feeling within them that maybe they will find difficult to explain, like searching for something you have lost. It may be a feeling of emptiness, a feeling of bewilderment, even if you are enjoying the happiest time of your life. It's a yearning for knowledge way beyond the earth's boundaries. Others just feel guided towards a more spiritual path to follow. Whatever feelings they experience it is all important that they are guided towards the correct group or circle so that they can receive the most appropriate form of guidance and training from an experienced medium on your earth.

When you first experience those subtle tendrils of thought being transmitted from spirit it can be bewildering you could experience these sensations:

Confusion: This is very common because many times when a person has not had an inkling that our world exists. They can be very confused as to where these thoughts or feelings are coming from.

Excitement: Could be felt by the person who has always wished to be able to connect with Spirit it would be normal for them to feel excited that it is now their time for development.

Apprehension: Maybe reaction of the person who likes to tread carefully through life it would be normal for them to feel apprehensive as to where this new path could lead them.

Rush: When a person finds they have found their 'gift' it is all too common for them to want to rush and tell others and demonstrate their gift before they are ready.

Every person on your earth has energies around them and these energies can vary from person to person. When joining a development group it is important that the blending of energies are compatible for that group, in order for everyone to work together in harmony. Harmonisation is the key factor in working with spirit. The idea of working with like-minded people in a group is that eventually you all experience the same oneness with spirit.

It is up to the experienced medium to explain how this can be realised within the group. The teaching and training one receives at the beginning is very important because this is the foundation for how your pathway will develop. It is also up to the teaching medium when it is decided for their pupil to expand beyond their group and share their gift with others. If they are sent out before they are ready it can have catastrophic consequences for the novice medium. As we mentioned earlier there is no need to rush, this is not a race.

The greatest reward is that your spiritual gift will give great comfort to others. Where confidence and experience is concerned, once our gift is discovered it is never taken away. There are times when spirit will feel they should step back away to give their medium some needed rest. Also, in our world egos do not exist.

If it transpires that a medium is working with their ego spirit will withdraw their energy until that medium realises that it is the humble person who makes the best advocate for spirit.

It is a long and arduous journey developing your spiritual gift, one that never ends. It continues when you shed your earthly body and join us back in the homeland of spirit. We hope it to be an enjoyable experience that will bring much comfort and peace. It takes time. Don't expect your gift to reach your expectations within a short period.

It is the most joyful experience when you can prove to another that you have concrete evidence that their loved ones are still very much around them in energy and thought; that their energies are sending love to all left behind on the earth. Our one aim is to give proof that life and the spiritual self is everlasting.

27

Trance and Direct Communication are two terms for the same form of mediumship. This is where spirit communicates with us using the voice of the medium to convey their words. This is achieved by creating a divine oneness with spirit. It is a blending of energies agreeable to both parties. Personally, I dislike the term Trance as it conjures up misleading images of being out of control. This very high level of mediumship is pure sweet harmony.

Spirit communicates on issues of their choosing. This may be about wars and upheavals or care for the planet, or to pass on knowledge during a teaching session. These communications are instigated by spirit. It is spirit that makes it known to the medium that they wish to communicate, not the other way round. More will be said on channelling in the next chapter.

Coming next:

In the next chapter we'll explain more about aspects of spirit. We will describe the process of connecting with spirit and invite you to attend a spiritual circle meeting within these pages.

Three

Tuning into Spirit

Your mind is the gateway to spirit. It is the entry point to spiritual awareness. By expanding consciousness you will be able to create a mental pathway to connect with the world of spirit. It's not easy. It requires dedication and perseverance. These words from spirit describe making this unique connection and the benefits it can bring:

When opening up your mind to spirit for the first time you are inviting in an amazing new world. It is not an easy journey at the beginning because your thoughts are clouded with fog and mist from your daily lives. Your new friends in spirit are there to guide you with dedication and perseverance. You will gradually take small steps along this pathway. On this journey you will learn how to connect with your new friends and guides. You will learn how to communicate with loved ones that have come back to our world and wish to let their grieving relatives and friends know that they are safe, happy and secure back in the homeland.

You will learn how to be at peace with yourself and be tolerant of those around you. You will learn that there is no need to be afraid of the transition everyone eventually has to take from the earth back to spirit. There is so much there waiting for you. The pathway will be a long and an enjoyable one. There is no rush, when things are done in a hurry they easily get lost. When things are done at a slow pace they are absorbed and secured in your mind and inner being.

This world is where your soul came from and is where your soul will go back to. Now you feel the time is right for you to enter an unknown world where you will meet your true self and make new friends. They will guide you, be there for you, never judge you and allow you to explore this new adventure at your own pace, allowing you to absorb all the wonders you will experience in our world.

The wonders we talk about are the simpler things in life that most people have forgotten about on their life's pathway such as wisdom, courage, knowledge, humility, clarity, forgiveness, to know yourself, to know others, to love yourself, to love others, to be understanding, to be empathetic, to open up your mind to allow yourself to think clearly about your human existence for the first time.

An Invitation to a Circle

You may have heard of people joining a spiritual circle to develop their skills. A circle is for anyone who has a desire to learn more and develop their spirituality. There are two types of circle. One open, the other closed. An open circle is 'open' to new people joining. It could be someone who is curious and wants to see for themselves what takes place. You should expect the atmosphere to be warm and welcoming. A closed circle has a number of regular members who are on a structured path to developing their psychic abilities. Experienced mediums manage the circle and decide what kind of activities will be the most beneficial for their members. This is to give you an idea of what happens at a circle meeting:

The Circle Begins

After chatting and relaxing with friends, the group sit together in the shape of a circle. The circle begins with exercises to calm the mind and dispel the stresses of the day.

1. The Opening Prayer

The medium leading the circle opens the meeting in prayer. The prayer gives thanks to spirit for the opportunity to gain wisdom and knowledge and for members to develop their gifts. The words of the prayer are flexible and chosen by the leader. The prayer would be dedicated to the divine light and welcome spirit for attending the meeting and for the love and learning that will follow.

2. Meditations to focus the mind and raise spiritual awareness

Once the prayer has been said, the circle members begin the process of putting their material lives to one side and to concentrate on their spiritual selves. Quiet meditation helps with this. Here are two techniques that do not require a mantra. These can be used to deflect the mind away from daily distractions and make you feel a whole lot better. Both techniques draw energy from the earth and down from spirit. The first is the Tree of Life:

The Tree of Life

Visualisation is a great way to take your mind away from everyday concerns. The Tree of Life is an ancient symbol that signifies immortality. The roots intertwining with the branches of the tree create one continuous circle of life. They make the eternal connection between heaven and earth. The Tree of Life can be the inspiration for a powerful meditation exercise to visualise the earth's magnetic force being drawn upward to meet the divine light descending from above. You may like to join in, take a moment to focus on the picture and see the interconnecting roots and branches around the central trunk of the tree. In your mind, you will become that living tree:

To begin, sit comfortably in a chair so that your feet, without shoes, are flat on the floor. Rest your hands on your thighs. Gently roll your shoulders and move your head and neck from side to side to release any muscular tension.

Close your eyes. Direct all your mental energy to your feet. Imagine you are as one with the earth. Visualise small tree roots sprouting from the soles of your feet and tiny roots are stemming from your toes.

See the roots burrow through the floor driving down, piercing the foundations of your house, going deeper and deeper into the soil, past rocks and stones penetrating down to the very centre of the earth.

All the while your roots are growing bigger and stronger soaking up earth's magnetic energy.

Energy travels upwards through your roots like streams of electric blue lava. You look down. Your ankles, calves and legs have entwined to form the single solid trunk of the tree. Bark crackles and forms a protective layer as your tree trunk widens through your hips getting thicker and taller going higher and higher leaving the ground way below you.

You look up. Your shoulders and arms have sprouted a thousand branches. Leaves have created a gloriously green canopy above you. You see a beam of light moving like a lightning strike through the canopy and down the trunk to blend seamlessly with earth's magnetic energy that is rising upwards along your trunk to meet at your solar plexus, the emotional centre of your being.

Hold that image. Feel the spiritual energy pulse through your body. Stay in the moment for as long as you wish. Slowly open your eyes and come back.

White Light Mediation is next:

White Light Meditation is a technique used within a medium's circle for the group members to unwind in preparation for raising the energies. It can also be linked directly with the seven chakras or energy centres in the body.

White Light Meditation involves picturing images of divine white light coursing through your body. The meditation begins with sitting with your back straight, feet apart and hands resting on your thighs. The palms of your hands can face upwards to receive energy from above. Take a few minutes to regulate your breathing in deep measured breaths. Exhaling air completely from your lungs and out into the room expels the body of air spent of energy. Try not to think of things in your everyday life. These thoughts will distract you, let them come and go without stopping inside your head. Dispel them. Tell them this is your time. They'll just have to wait. You're moving into a spiritual state of mind away from the physical world.

Close your eyes.

Imagine a concentrated cone of divine white light hovering above the crown of your head. Then switch your attention to the earth beneath your feet. Draw up magnetic energy from the core of the planet. The two energies high and low meet and blend beautifully. Now think of the divine white light from above lowering to touch the top of your head. You may feel a tingling at first as it touches your hair like static electricity. Moving slowly downwards, it covers your head and the nape of your neck. The healing glow expands across your shoulders and slips in gentle waves to your cheek and down your back warming and relaxing, warming and relaxing, getting lower and lower to the base of your spine. Then focus on your thighs, knees, calves, ankles, feet and toes, soothing and relaxing, soothing and relaxing. Your whole body is embraced and sealed in divine loving light.

Hold that image. Allow the light to suffuse through your whole body inside and out. After a moment open your eyes and come back. When you feel relaxed the next step is to raise energies using the chakras.

3. Chakras

Spirits operate at a higher mental energy level than we do. Once circle members have quietened their minds and entered a more receptive state, a process begins to raise their collective energies to narrow that gap. Heightening the vibrations is achieved by energising the centres in the body that are pathways to the mind. It is believed that the chakras provide this pathway. You may have noticed that all you've been reading so far in the book concerns the power of thought energy from the mind.

Each individual chakra position has a physical and spiritual resonance as they work together. Think of them as seven steps to raising consciousness. Each has its own colour; together they form the colours of the rainbow. The numbered position on the body and our seven colours of the rainbow guide is:

No	Colour	Position
1	Red	Pelvic area
2	Orange	Below the navel
3	Yellow	Solar plexus
4	Green	At the heart centre
5	Indigo/Blue	At the throat
6	Violet/ Purple	Third Eye – in the centre of your forehead
7	White /Silver	Top centre of your head – the crown

4. Inspirational Words and Messages

Opening the chakras builds energy and creates the optimum conditions for the two worlds of earth and spirit to come together. It also sets the scene for members of the circle to develop their own spiritual skills. Giving an inspirational address is one exercise. Some will stand behind their chairs and are given a word to stimulate their thoughts and prompt a message from spirit. More experienced mediums may have already been contacted by their spirit guides who wish to pass on a message to the gathering for them all or for a particular person.

5. Training Session

You never stop learning. When you first actively engage and sit in a circle it could take some time to make a breakthrough.

Spirit knows when the time is right. Enlightenment could be gradual at first with you sensing that you are becoming more intuitive. There are no ticking clocks in spirit. Spirit dictates the pace. The whole atmosphere is mutually supportive. One aim could be to learn the identity of your spirit guide. Your guide would have been with you since birth and will be by your side during your time on earth. Your guide is your closest friend in your spiritual development. You will also have your own spirit animal.

6. The Closing

The circle is reformed after a training session. Open Chakras, energy centres, are now mentally closed one by one. The energy that was at a peak dissipates and is directed back to the earth. The circle hears the closing prayer. The wording is flexible and given from the heart for example:

"Divine gracious spirit, we thank you for drawing close this evening. We ask you to spread the healing light of love from head to head around the world in the hope that one day the world will come together in peace. Amen."

This last chapter has been about tuning in and connecting with spirit.

This message was received by Janet on the theme of friendship:

Tuning in and connecting with spirit is an enjoyable experience After all, we are your friends and when friends meet it is a joyous occasion. Like all friendships there is the first meeting that gradually strengthens between people and becomes a common link which they all share that leads to respect and trust within that friendship. True friendship never dies.

Friendship with spirit has many avenues. It is the bonding process with the person on the earth and their spirit guide to harmonise between one another, and then to establish which pathway they would like to walk along together. Spirit would not make anyone walk along a pathway that wouldn't be suited to them. It is up to the person to decide with guidance from the spirit friend which avenue they would like to explore. Because my friends that is what you are doing, exploring our world and way of existence. Upon doing so, you are gathering knowledge from our world and transmitting it to your world, spreading comfort and love to all who will listen.

It's common at times when a person is developing the bond and gift with spirit that the pupil can experience despondency as to their progression. They can feel they are not connecting with their guides. This is natural to feel like this, it is a common thought on your earth that everything comes to them rapidly. It is a slow process which will eventually happen where the knowledge that has been gained is firmly cemented in the mind, therefore enabling you to continue on your spiritual path.

Joining groups and circles to connect with our world takes time, dedication, practice and patience. There is no need for anyone to rush the wonderful experience that can be established between your world and ours. Just imagine you are walking slowly upon a path that will eventually lead you to the most peaceful place of existence. It will be a path where you will make many new friends, both in your world and ours. You will also be able to bring both the worlds *together by proving existence of many loved ones who have departed from your world. You will also experience the love and warmth from the healing powers given by spirit.*

Blue Flame gave some practical advice on how to connect with your guide. This advice centres on the blending of energies and the relationship between a medium and their guide:

At the moment you are writing about the connection of the medium with their guides. It is an important subject where it is imperative for the novice medium to understand if their intentions are for the smooth pattern of their pathway. When a person chooses to join a circle their first thought is how long will it take me to tune in and be able to give messages to people? Will I be able to see and hear spirit with clarity or will I be sensing their energies around me, either way when will I be able to give proof of the afterlife?

It is a human trait that people want everything to happen quickly. They become impatient if they feel they are not progressing at a steady rate. The first rule for connection with their guide is relaxation and not to expect dramatic changes with their minds or energies. After they have mastered how to relax and they feel comfortable then the next phrase is to become aware of very subtle changes with their energies. This allows the guides to be able to blend their energies with the medium. Once this has been established they might experience subtle movement around their person. This could be as a light breeze in the air, slight touching of the skin or slight pressure mainly around the head area. This is your guide's way of introducing themselves.

It is important on your earth to have a label or name given to them. Many spirits will oblige with this information, not by shouting it out with clarity but by subtle thoughts that will be transmitted through their energies into the mind of the medium. There are some guides who feel it is not necessary for a name to be given in this incidence they will mainly give a physical sign so their medium would be in no doubt that they have a connection.

Once the novice has settled into the rhythm of regular attendance and discipline then they will gradually start becoming aware of the information that is being transmitted to them. At first they may sense, see or hear a presence, this could be the energy of a person wishing to make contact. This presence may only last for seconds then fade, over time the energies will stay for a longer period. It doesn't happen overnight it can take a few years of your time on earth just to get that first feeling of energy, it is a slow process.

One of the golden rules for the new medium to understand is the importance of regular attendances to the circle and also the relaxation and blending when they are in their homes. This does not have to be one of deep meditation, although some people find this to be helpful. Each of you has different ways which is comfortable for you to blend in with the energies of spirit. It is for the person to experiment with each method until they find which one is suitable and comfortable for them.

The main purpose is to become compatible with the guides energies. One method can be to sit in a chair in a quietened room with a clear mind and talk silently to your guide. At first the medium might not be aware of any energies surrounding them, given time this will happen. This is the *beginning of blending and harmonisation with the guide. The medium may feel uncomfortable talking in their mind to nothingness. We can assure you that there will always be the guide there it takes time for the communication to flow between the two energies. It is Important for the medium to understand they are not talking to themselves, the voice of their guide can resemble their own voice. It will normally come from the same place in their mind at all times, with practice and experience they will know the difference when it is their guide or when they are answering themselves.*

Another method can be one of sitting in a quietened room with low music and eyes closed. If the music is too loud this can interfere with the flow of energies, spirits like the sound of music. It is a calming influence for the medium and also allows spirit to blend-in easier.

Some people may find it more relaxing and suitable for them to lay down either on a bed or the floor. Whatever method is chosen it is important that the place where they are relaxing is quite and comfortable in temperature and free of any disturbances from other people or outside noise.

Whatever method is chosen the guidelines are the same. Converse with your guide get to know how their energies work. Never be afraid to question them. Trust them. They will never let you down. If these rules are followed then the medium will gradually start to become aware that the discipline and dedication they have shown is resulting in the harmonisation of a long lasting friendship with their guide. It is not a quick process it can take many years to get to the point where the medium and guides energies are flowing in perfect harmony.

In the previous chapter Janet described her experience of providing clairvoyance messages during a church service. To close this chapter Running Water would like to describe what it is like from their 'other world' viewpoint to witness a circle meeting:

We would like to describe the meeting to you as we are witnessing it or as we 'see it'. We will use the terms for you as the earth group and for us the spirit group.

After members of the earth group are assembled and have settled themselves within the quietness, the energies of the spirit group gather above their heads. There are many of us in the spirit group and we all have different roles. Only a chosen few are selected at any one time to channel their energies toward a particular medium who they wish to converse through.

Each member present on the earth group will have the energies of a spirit directed at them. In a meeting such as this, it may not necessarily be their own guide although their energies would be around you. This is because there would be a relaxed atmosphere of spectators watching other mediums in your earth group channel messages from us rather than working themselves.

Lights emanating from the auras of the earth group would become noticeable to us. You would all illuminate from the earth sending your energies in our direction so we can blend together. Your lights in yesterday's meeting were pulsating light and energy in a way where we were all linked in a compatible way thus allowing the spiritual energy to flow with fluidity. If members of a circle or group are not gelling together, or there is disharmony within the group, then the light and energy become weak thus affecting the flow of the group causing the members to have a disappointing meeting.

This is how it works. My energies always take the lead when Janet is sitting. Once the prayer has been said my energies blend with Janet's energies. For us, this is an easy process because this has been done over numerous times and we are well practiced. When the conversation begins her light becomes more vibrant. This causes a surge of energy which will filter its way through the channel of light that encircles the earth group. Because you all have blended well with each other, your lights become charged with increased energy enabling the connection with the spirit group to strengthen as a result.

From the spirit side we are witnessing lights of all different strengths. Imagine looking at the sunlight shining upon the water where the breeze is creating a rippling effect giving the impression of dancing lights where some are brighter than others that is how we can explain the picture from spirit side. When I am satisfied that all the energies are settled and have conversed enough then the go ahead is given for communication to begin.

Whilst this is going on we have a strong circle of spirit guides protecting the meeting from the spirit side warding off any stray or mischievous entities that might be curious as to what is going on. We exist in a very fine atmosphere and it is imperative that we have maximum protection during the meetings. Our mediums are precious to us it is our duty to keep you all protected.

It is my decision who will converse through Janet bearing in mind her energy is the strongest, therefore we allow the stronger of the spirits to blend in with her energies. Who is *chosen to come and converse? This my friend will vary from one meeting to the next. It all depends on who is present on the earth side and what they have in their minds. I often hear conversations that have taken place before the meeting begins. Sometimes I feel I should contribute to the conversation. This can be a surprise to group members as they weren't expecting spirit to be listening.*

We try to keep each meeting different from the next. We like to include topics which we feel would be of interest to the sitters at the time or my friend as you would have already understood, this could be just general conversation. It is our role to keep the interaction flowing between the two worlds. If the interest is waning then the energy will start to decrease causing tiredness to the active medium.

We on the spirit side are always busy with the continuous build-up of energy flowing from the earth side. It is pulsing living light that exists while the meeting takes place. After a certain amount of time we witness the energy slightly fading and the light dim, this confirms to us that the mediums are tiring and is an indication for me to close the circle.

When the meeting comes to an end, the closing prayer is said on the spirit and earth side. The energy generated by the meeting becomes ethereal and evaporates on the earth side. A layer of protection is then placed over every person. The meeting is ended. Fresh energies begin to build for the next.

We wanted to make a point about spirit protecting the meeting. When people on the earth side meet together they need time to enter a spiritual frame of mind and to put the pressures and stresses of their daily lives behind them. Being human it's so easy to get sidetracked. The protection of spirit is to help us banish these thoughts and rid our minds of them. You know that our emotions, good and bad, govern our thoughts and it is thought energy that makes the connection with spirit. When Running Water uses the words 'stray or mischievous entities' he is referring to negative thoughts that do the sidetracking. Spirit shields us from this negativity.

Running Water's message reinforces the dedication and degree with which spirit works with us. If you consider that we are all spirits on different sides of life, this positive interaction doesn't seem so strange. Ultimately we are working together. We on the earth side are at a certain point in our development. A stage that Running Water would have experienced during his lifetime as a Plains Indian. Remember that spirit guides were once flesh and blood like us.

Running Water wanted to continue by expanding our knowledge of the channelling process as it affects his interaction with Janet.

He explains how guides in the spirit world follow a routine when they are approved by him to connect of Janet's channelling talents. The first thing is for them to introduce themselves. It gives Running Water enormous satisfaction to hear his words spoken out loud by Janet here on the earth plane, but also to have his words recorded in writing for you to read:

Hello Steve, It's Running Water,

When a spirit guide channels messages through Janet their first words are to identify themselves by name. This is for the benefit of the person receiving the message and is done in a similar way that I began this message. This is done so that the listener on earth has instant recognition of who is speaking to them. This instantly makes the listener feel relaxed and able to address the communicator by name making the conversations flow more easily. If the introductions are not established at the beginning of the conversations then the listener can disturb the sensitive energy or vibrations because they are trying to conjure up a vision of who the visiting speaker is.

In your physical life you come across many people, on first meeting you can immediately see who you are conversing with. At times it can just be a person who you are talking to in a queue or just sitting in a waiting room. At these times it's not important for names to be exchanged. The chances are your paths will not cross again. Then there are other scenarios where it is necessary or important for names or titles to be exchanged. It makes the information flow a lot easier between the two parties, plus it would be easier if your paths were to cross again in the future. Then you would instantly recognise each other by remembering their names and what they looked like. This allows you to prepare yourself and adjust your thoughts and energies. With friends, not only would you be familiar with their name but also their energies and personalities allowing easy communication even where there is no visual sight because you would feel comfortable with their energies.

This is how it is with spirit. You can liken it to the blind person on your earth. The blind cannot see the person but they would be recognisable to them if the speaker was male or female through their voice. Other than that they would be doing guesswork to whom they were conversing. If they gave a name or title can make all the difference because then that person or energy would instantly become recognisable in the communication between them.

In the same way, you cannot see us when we are conversing with you. We use the voice of the channeller. It can vary from one medium to another as to the tones of the vocal cords which are used. We use certain tones like a gentler tone or harsher tone, quieter, louder or deep, slow or fast. At the very start of our writings to you we were very aware of the fact that the energies flowing through Janet would be the personalities of the spirit dictating the letters.

When spirit speaks through her the individual personalities are given expression by the way she talks or moves her head or makes gestures to capture the character of the spirit. She would be feeling their emotions and would know almost instantly who they were. Once the letters reached you that emotional element would have been lost to you because they were just words. Any humour would have been dismissed, it was important that each letter was signed by the writer so you would become familiar with who they were and the way they wrote.

Now you have regular meetings with us you are gradually blending in with our energies thus making it easier for you to recognise us through our personalities, although it is still difficult for you to instantly recognise who is speaking. Once the name has been given to you are instantly at ease and conversations can commence with fluidity.

We are also very aware that people like to have a description of the spirit who they are conversing with. It can make communication more real to the human spirit. Visualisation plays an important part in your daily lives *unless you are visually impaired then verbal description would become more important.*

In my group we try to give you as much information as possible on each spirit that communicates through Janet. This is either done verbally or from a descriptive personality, meaning it's possible to create an image of someone through their speech, their mannerisms, their choice of subjects and the conversations they have. To us it's not that important to visualise matter.

We only see and are attracted to light.

Maybe we are at an advantage my friend for when our energies blend with your energies on the earth the knowing is instantaneous whereas you have to take time and effort to know and familiarise yourself with a person. You have to trust your own instincts and at times can be disappointed and disheartened when you have been let down by an emotion that betrayed you. When we blend energies we have certainty.

I enjoy the concept of being able to communicate to you through the written word as well as the verbal communication which we enjoy. It creates more of a familiarity between our energies enabling the bonding and blending to be cemented eventually as one, thus creating a state of harmony where our energies flow together which is important for future work that is before you.

It is also important from our side and your side that all communication is understood and should any misunderstandings occur that they are quickly settled. It is a human trait that at times can misinterpret information which flows from our side. We give you our honest view and only information what you need to know rather then what you want to know. You will have many conversations with us over time which will be ones of friendship and guidance, through every conversation. There will always be something of which will stay within your memory for future use. There is always a teaching element through every communication between us and that will carry on when it is your turn to come back and rejoin with us.

My friend I hope this has been of some interest to you, Running Water.

Did you notice the sentence: *We only see and are attracted to light?* That answers a big question in many minds. Spirits sense energy in the form of light that emanates from the crown chakra position at the top of the head. The light shines brighter the more we show love and are more in-tune we are with spirit. For spirit, our light is their homing beacon. We are not being watched and recorded every day of our lives. To answer the unasked question; private times are always private, if you know what I mean.

Coming next:

The next chapter is dedicated to learning more about Spirit Guides, Guardian Angels, Angels and Archangels. You'll be amazed at the depth of the celestial support system that's on constant call to help and support us.

Four

Spirit Guides, Helpers, Doorkeepers and Angels

Spirit is always at least one step ahead of us. As we were about to finish writing the last chapter this message arrived for this new one. It is about the lifelong relationship between a spirit guide and the human spirit they are partnered with. These words are from Black Feathers he uses the general term 'medium' to mean someone on earth and the link with their guide:

> *The role of the guide is one of love and friendship. They are there to help, guide and protect. They will never judge. They would never take their chosen medium down a road of which they would be uncomfortable. They would never fill their medium's thoughts with ego or with thoughts that would cause harm to others. They are your friends; the bonding of a friendship lasts until the two energies meet back again in our world.*

They would never let you down, even if the medium would become disheartened with the development between the two energies, which is natural. On your earth, time is of importance, people want things to happen quickly. When the process is slow it can cause frustration on the earth's side, but the guide will still be there at your side with an abundance of love and patience.

The guide would have taken many years to harmonise and get to know the energies with whom they are working and have to take into account the personality, lifestyle, setbacks and traumas that a medium would face. It is the role of the guide to be able to know when the time is right for that person to develop the gifts that they have been given in order for it to be the right time for them to progress. No guide would push to the extent that it would cause mental or physical harm to their medium.

Guides do not control their medium. It is a partnership of love and friendship. The blending of energies can work as one and be the best friend that would never let you down. This is natural in your world. The guides understand for they have also at one point been in an earthly existence. They have chosen this role. They are spirit messengers whose only aim is to help disperse the love and light from our world to yours.

Spirit guides have lived on earth. Guides may have experienced a number of earthly visits each one at a different human situation, in different time periods and in different circumstances. As they have learned during their lifetimes so you will learn during your lifetime. You have one principal guide assigned to you. They will be with you from conception to passing.

At times your number one guide will have other supporting guides to help you. Talk to your guides. Think of them when you're feeling down. Thank them when you're exultant. Ask their opinion when making decisions. They are there for you. Include them in your true friendship group. Your guide and guardian angel are your greatest supporters. Black Feathers continues to describe the role of helpers. These are spirits who are at the early stages of learning and development in the spirit world:

Helpers or Scouts

Every guide has many helpers. The role of a helper is to be able to give influential energy and information at specific times in a person's life. When they feel they have given as much informative information and can't help any further, they move on to help another person. Their work is invaluable. It is the same in your world. Certain people come into your life at times for a short period but when they have gone they stay forever etched into your memory for the part they played during that time. The helper would continuously touch the energy of the physical form to give encouragement and guidance as a memory. It is also possible for the helper to return to the physical being many years after just to give that nudge again into the right direction. Helpers are also known as scouts in the spirit world as they are in training to assist other more advanced guides. They are sent to retrieve information from the halls of learning and report back with answers. This is part of their development.

Door Keepers or Gate Keepers:

These spirits are probably the most protective of all. Their role is to guard and protect the energy field around each person to keep any negative energies from invading the auric field of the medium. Every living being has a guide who has been there since birth. It is the role of a guide to help that person through every pathway that life has put them on. If the person does not believe or recognise our existence then the help we can give them is of little use. We do not give up. We carry on continuing with our help although it can become very frustrating for us when we are witnessing that person continuously making mistakes and ignoring our help there is little for us to do, except to continue to be with their energy.

A door keeper will mainly work with people who have a solid belief in our existence and who will allow us to work with them. It's important for the physical form who is working with spirit to have that extra solid protection. This is not to say that a door keeper will ignore any other physical form. They will choose any physical energy they feel will need their protection.

We are your friends, guardians, angels and door keepers we are all part of a single loving energy. We guide and direct. Our work combined together is important for both of our worlds.

Black Feathers Cheyenne Warrior

Angels in High Places

Angels are divine. They are light beings. Angles are emissaries of the Divine Spirit, Holy Spirit or God depending on whichever form of address you're most comfortable with. Whatever your belief system it is the same God, the same divine light. Angels are a permanent presence. You have your own guardian angel who is only a thought away. Angels are constantly on-duty, caring, protecting and looking after you.

These are Black Feather's words:

The Ministry of Angels

Is an Angel a guide? Is a guide an Angel? What's the difference? These are questions that are continuously being asked of us. An angel is a spirit that has transcended from the divine light to help and protect us. They are light in the purest form and are sent to help people in moments of extreme distress. They can come in many different categories from the Archangel Gabriel through to the angelic spirit sent to help a person on your earth who is suffering from living a material life.

Imagine a vast empty space where the intensity of light is so great that it would be impossible for any physical form to view through unprotected eyes. Also imagine air that is so light that you could float. Imagine a feeling of the utmost euphoria that you could burst with love. All these sensations combined together are the energy of an angel. This is possible only because this energy is pure spirit that has been untouched by any negativity.

Angels have many roles. They can pluck a person from the edge of returning to our world because it would not have been time for that person to return. They can help many when they have lost a loved one and feel that there is nothing left for them to continue to live. They can help the person on earth who has been bullied into believing they are worthless.

No one on your earth is worthless. Everybody has a role to play. It's how they play their part that matters.

My friend we must not forget the role of an angel which every parent or guardian should be aware of and that is to be there when their beloved infant has been cruelly taken away from them. Whatever the circumstances, the love and affection these newly returned child spirits are embraced in is beyond any energy or love that is given in your material world. Angels are also there to help any returning spirit back to our world especially those who have been taken quickly and traumatically.

As well as being assigned to you during your lifetime your guardian angel is a member of the Ministry of Angels. The ministry is there when you need particular, specialised help in different areas of your life. You can call in the Ministry to help you prepare for a job interview, or give you courage when meeting someone for the first time. Basically, they are there to call whenever you need them. They are your 'A' team.

Earth Angels

Angels can and do visit our world. They don't stay. They're here to work their angelic magic then return to spirit. They can make their present felt in one of two ways. They may take human form to appear in person to help someone. I have heard stories from reliable people who are not given to fantasy. One encounter was from a friend whose car had broken down on a country road in winter. He was looking down at the engine trying to fix the problem. A man stepped out of a van and offered to help. He asked my friend to get behind the wheel and turn the ignition. The engine coughed and started. Full of thanks, my friend got out the car. There was no sign of the man, no sound of the van driving away, no tracks arriving or leaving in the snow. When he thought about it he didn't hear a van arriving either.

Earth Angels also help by saving someone from harm without evidence of their presence. You may have heard accounts of people who were either felt being pushed or pulled to avoid an accident. It is as if someone had grabbed their coat and pulled them back onto the pavement or sidewalk to avoid being struck by a speeding car or lorry. One minute they were stepping into the street, the next they were safe without being conscious of what just happened. Angels use a sound or a blast of air or a sudden shout to distract and stop someone from walking into danger, for example to avoid a piece of masonry or scaffolding falling from a building, or a shout to warn them of something in their path like an open manhole cover. Again they have no idea where the warning came from.

Archangels Michael, Raphael and Gabriel are three of the best known. In early religious writings, the male gender was commonly ascribed to Archangels. However, as they are divine beings they are beyond this earthly description as they transcend gender. However, for the purpose of these descriptions we will use the conventional terms.

Here's a fuller introduction to these three Archangels:

Michael: Whose name means 'like God', is considered to be the leader of the Angels. As such he is powerful and known for his love and protection. You can think of him and ask his support in making difficult decisions and helping you move forward in life. Call on him and he will come to you aid. He will help banish fear and doubt.

Gabriel: In Christianity he is known as a messenger of God. If you are anxious and need help to calm yourself or to increase your confidence levels he will be there by your side. As communication is his special area he helps writers and teachers.

Raphael: Healing of mind body and spirit is Archangel Raphael's particular area of influence. He is a touchstone of creativity to help boost your intuition and inspiration. Thinking of Raphael helps restore calm and peace, relieve stress and promote healing.

We have just received this new message direct from source It concerns the Sisters of Mercy. These are not linked to the earthbound religious organisations known as the Sisters of Mercy. These are the originals beyond the clouds. They include doctors, nurses and carers among their number:

The Sisters of Mercy play an important role in our spirit world. The majority of them work within the realms near to your earth plane. They are there to help the transition from your world to ours. These are spirits that, when they were in an earthly incarnation, would have chosen the pathway working for God, the infinite Light; a role which takes them along a route of caring for others. They would have spent the majority of their lifetime on earth caring for the sick and suffering. It is a natural instinct within their souls to carry out this work when they return to the homeland.

Eventually every person on earth comes to the end of their lifetime. There is no set length of time for this, for some it could be minutes, hours, a few years or much longer. When the time comes for your spirit to be detached from the earthly body the ending is personal for everyone. There are many ways in which a lifetime is ended, for some it can be a relief, if a body has suffered much distress through illness. For that person it is a blessing to be relieved from all pain and suffering. Some lives are ended very tragically and many can be frightened by the fear of the unknown. Whatever the reason or cause of their parting, we in our world would like to stress to everyone that there is no fear to coming home.

The Sisters of Mercy are there to help make the transition from your world back to ours with as much tranquillity as they can. They continue to care for that spirit for as long as it takes. They act as mothers would to a new-born child. The love is continuously given in order for the spirit to come to terms with the new environment in which they find themselves.

Their love and attention is endless. They are there to guide each new spirit towards the eternal light.

Shortly after Janet received that message another came through. This is heart-breaking, but will be a comfort for those who have lived through or are still living with the aftermath of this tragedy:

To lose a child back to the world of spirit is one of the most traumatic experiences a parent has to face. There are no words of comfort that can be given at such a sad time. Parents experience a heartbreaking turmoil of emotions, sadness that seems to have no end, anger, rage, confusion as to why their beloved offspring was taken away from them and fear that their precious gift is left alone without their loving arms to hold them.

We would like to expel that fear with the truth that for each and every infant there is a band of angels waiting to hold their spirit in love, warmth and protection. These angels are light in the purest form. Their entire existence has been one that has never touched the earth's atmosphere. They are completely formed from the purest of Light. For the earth child that has just been returned to our world to be received by these precious angels, the experience is one of extreme happiness and joy. The angels are there to receive the spirit with an abundance of love with the assurance that the child's soul is filled with happiness.

At the same time that this transition is taking place in spirit, there are experienced angels who have chosen to work with the departed child's guardians who have remained on the earth and are experiencing grief and sadness of their loss. The angels are there to help lessen the shock and sadness, the love from these angels is generated towards the energy of the grieving relatives thus giving them the courage to carry on.

Combining the energies with these angels and the Sisters of Mercy will enable the grieving relatives to move forward with the acceptance that the one they are grieving over is happy, safe, secure, at peace and very much loved.

Here is a profile of Black Feathers a respected teaching guide and member of the core group of eight:

My friend we understand the importance to you of our earthly existence. We are happy that our names and characters are to be mentioned in your books it will be of much interest to many who are reading the written word. There are many people on your earth who have a great interest in the Native American Indian.

Over the centuries on your earth there have been many stories or tales written about our tribes, our traditions, our conquests. My time on the earth was long, peaceful and happy. There were many hardships that would have interrupted the course of my lifetime these would have been expected. I was no chief of a tribe, just an ordinary person living amongst many who through the years of my life would have gained much knowledge and wisdom and it was a given right to pass that on. I would have taken a wife and bore her children, two passed in infancy and two lived beyond my years. The territory of which we lived would have been hot and humid through the summer months and cold during the winter months, the plains where we stayed were vast.

Unlike the time you now find yourself living in where you have many disturbances from your modern world where it is impossible to even think without having noise or disruption of some sort. We had a quiet peaceful existence and valued time with family and friends. We would have passed stories on from our forefathers, sang and performed rites that kept us protected and taught the younger members of the tribes our ways of existence.

My friend that time of my life was many hundreds years ago when the people living in that part of the world were native to the country. This was before settlers came and eventually took over. My language would have been different from the tongue which you speak. I would have derived from Cheyenne territory.

My friend this is but a very short version of my time on your earth,

Black Feathers.

Coming next:

Life is eternal. How does our passage of time on earth fit into the spiritual cycle?

Five

The Spiritual Cycle of Life

You could be forgiven for thinking your life began at birth. That's certainly true of your life on earth, this time around. The thing is; you were alive in spirit before that. Coming from spirit was the starting point of the life you're experiencing now. Each of us may have had several past incarnations. Each one would be a stage in your learning cycle. Spiritual life is everlasting. Spirit use the concept of incarnation to explain the life cycle that continually turns and evolves until we are pure of spirit. When we reach that point we become as one with the divine light. We become as one with God.

Time in the spirit world does not exist. This is difficult for humans to comprehend; we who live by the ticking clock of mortality. We pace ourselves by the seven ages of man from birth to death, from start to finish in our earthly state. With each incarnation we are challenged to discover more about who we are. Your spirit moves closer to enlightenment, closer to the divine with each earthly encounter. It's as if spirit design a fresh new earthly experience with each incarnation. It will be a new challenge every time you visit earth's atmosphere designed to improve the core of your spiritual being. Before you were born on earth, you would have made the choice to return for another incarnation, one where you would be living life in a different way.

A single sunflower will help explain the spiritual incarnation concept. At the beginning of the cycle, the divine light created a pod of pure energy. This new creation of energy is you. This is where the sunflower comes in. Visualise a single sunflower plant with all its beautiful yellow and gold leaves surrounding a circular head comprising hundreds of seeds pressed together. Imagine that each individual seed represents a different aspect of your personality a different facet of your being. Each seed has its own characteristics. It is part of the whole but separate.

Imagine that over many incarnations each seed, every individual particle or pod of energy, experiences life on earth. Each seed has a different pathway and lives a different lifetime before returning to the sunflower. When the seed returns it takes its original place amongst the hundreds of seeds in the head of the flower. It is not one seed returning time and time again, but different seeds with each separate incarnation. Every returning seed, every particle of energy brings back new learning and knowledge. Eventually the one flower is made whole again and is totally transformed to become pure of spirit and a particle of God.

With every incarnation the awakening is through your intuition. You sense, you feel, you begin to comprehend these hidden elements. Intuition sparks the desire to learn more about your character. This may come about at a stressful time in your life or on losing a loved one. At times like these our souls cries out for a force of good and understanding to run to our aid, to ease our pain. Alternately, your awakening could be from an intensely spiritual experience that is your dawn of realisation.

This is spirit talking to you, in your mind, in your thoughts. By reading this you're already on the quest to learn more about spirit and yourself. Awakening leads to wanting to learn more about the role and purpose of spirit. Many choose to follow conventional religions that have evolved from the teachings of others here on earth. Following spirituality in the form we are describing does not stem from a religious sect. Spirituality has never started a war, caused a death, started an insurrection, instigated trouble, created disharmony or sparked racial genocide in the name of religion. At birth human spirit is pure. It is the impact of living your life that shapes character and personality. In broad terms it is a combination of those two factors we hear about namely, nature and nurture. Nature is your inherent biological make-up and received through genes and passed on by family bloodlines. This reflects aspects such as height, weight, and vulnerability to illness. Nurture is a child's physical environment, the parental influences and formative experiences that influence character and personality.

This is how Black Feathers describes the spiritual cycle. He begins by describing how a human spirit returns to the homeland to the world of spirit after passing. He's chosen this return to spirit as the starting point of the spiritual cycle:

Life is eternal and everlasting. Upon returning to the homeland the newly returned spirit is looked after with an abundance of love and understanding now that their earthly life has now ended. Some will feel they would have liked to have stayed for a longer period of time. Some would be ready for their return. However they felt upon returning, each is cared and looked after as if it is their first time back in our world.

You are aware of the processes each spirit follow when they return. What is not commonly known is that the spirit has to be able to adjust back into our world without a body, without a physical form. They are immediately happy and at peace within their mind. It takes time for the adjustment to take place. It takes time for them to shed the memories and presence of life in a physical form, all this is done and achieved within a veil of love and protection. Once the spirit has gone through this process (which my friend can take many earth years to accomplish) then they are faced with a decision which is what next. Do they allow their minds to continuously evolve towards the eternal flame of light? Do they become pupils and learn with the prospect of becoming guides themselves and working with a medium in a physical body? Do they visit and stay within the halls of learning allowing their minds to become a library of knowledge, or do they wish to return back to your earth to once again experience life in a completely different incarnation?

Once they have made their decision then the necessary steps are taken for their chosen pathway. It is not done lightly. Many measures are taken to prepare the spirit for their chosen journey. You can liken it as a child in your earth being prepared for school. It is done in gradual spiritual steps.

How does a spirit choose their new life? This depends my friend on how they were in their previous existence. Much thought goes into returning. It's common on your earth for people to speak of karma, what goes around comes around. If you were bad in one life would you be good in the next and vice-versa? If you were selfish and thought of no one but yourself would you be humble? Every situation will have reverse to it. If you had physical disabilities would you be perfectly formed? If you were a ruler with extreme power would you return as someone who is servile and put upon? If you only lived for a few hours or a few years would you live a life of longevity? If you were male would you be female? If you lived in poor conditions would you experience the opposite? All these questions will be decided.

The point of return for any spirit is probably the most difficult pathway for them to choose. The reason being is that each life led on your earth is for the spirit to learn lessons as to how every aspect of your emotions can be explored and understood. There is no such thing as a person born without emotions. They are there in every human soul it is how they are used, it is how the mind operates.

We have spoken before on this subject they will choose their lifestyle before they are back on the earth. Upon returning to earth their memories of past lives would be erased from their new minds. From that point onwards the different elements of their new existence such as their geographical position, genetics and status amongst their peers, every aspect that will have an impact on how a new existence is to be lived will be determined.

The important message here my friend is that life is eternal whatever path you choose. Life on the earth is an *experience which many choose to repeat time and time again until they felt they have exhausted every aspect of human emotion. Each return will be pure and clear with memories or disturbances from previous lives being erased. It is like a blank canvas waiting for the artist to shape a new story. Every life that returns is precious and to be cherished. The aim is to give and receive love and to respect your fellow man. My friend we can only hope and try that one day that will be achieved.*

Closing the earth cycle

As this lifetime ends your spiritual life continues. When this incarnation reaches its final stage you will keep your earthly personality and identity as you pass back into spirit. This is how White Cloud describes those moments:

When the transition takes place from the earth to the homeland a spirit keeps their personality and identity. It stays with them in order for them to be easily recognised when making communication with the ones they have left behind. As been explained once the spirit embarks upon their own personal journey they become unattached to the earth's atmosphere and evolve further into the realms, thus embarking upon a pathway of their choosing.

After volumes of time many choose the pathway towards the divine light, this is where that particular spirit would have gone through all the processes involved within our world, which would include the cleansing of the spirit, revisiting the life they had led and thus atoning for any mistakes that they would have made. These spirits they would be enveloped

*within the peace and tranquillity and continue to ascend
towards the divine light.*

Another spiritual cycle begins…

As one cycle ends another begins. The cleansing process
upon returning to the spirit world involves a debriefing of
what your human spirit learnt while on earth. Imagine it's like
a spiritual performance assessment when everything you've
experienced is captured in your book of life. Unless you've
done something terrible or repeatedly committed crimes
against humanity this process is supportive and loving.
Everyone who passes into spirit continues their journey
toward the divine light, learning and evolving toward the
godhead.

If a spirit chooses to come back to continue their learning
process on earth there is much thought and preparation is
put into their incarnation. A spirit experiences more with
each visit to the earth plane. It is a continuing cycle of
development with every earthly situation.

These are the words of Blue Flame for us to pass on this
added wisdom to you. You will notice that his words are in
harmony with Black Feathers:

*People choose their own destinies despite many thinking that
their life has already been mapped out when they were still in
spirit waiting for their return.*

*It's true that when the spirit decide to make another
journey to your earth there are many processes they have to
go through before they have another incarnation. We will call
it the clearing halls, just like the halls of learning it is a mass of
energy of the lightest form. There will be experienced spirits*

who would have trained for the role they are conducting which is to make sure that every spirit returning to the earth is ready for what awaits them.

They would take into account the type of lifestyle they would have endured during their previous incarnations. They would make sure that the returning spirit is cleansed of any of their previous life's existence. No spirit returns with any blemishes from a previous existence they would have to be pure spirit to start on yet another journey.

The reasons spirit choose to return is so that they can experience a life in different ways, geographical positions are important, living life in different parts of your world can bring along challenges for many. Your world has yet to find the balance of equal spirituality for all. There are countries where many are still suffering hardship from events that would have happened an age ago, countries where they have been and are still being ravaged by wars, countries that manage to survive through the destruction of extreme environmental episodes and countries that are not overly wealthy but balanced enough so that the people living within those boundaries can live a near peaceful existence.

Then we come to the different lifestyles of which there are many. If a person had previously led a wealthy existence that would have come to them through easy means; then they might choose to lead the life style of one who has to work extremely hard in order to make ends meet. If they had led a life where they would have been mean to the people around them; then they would come back into a life of the opposite.

Spirits returning to earth have made their choices of what type of lifestyle they will lead. However, it all hinges what kind of person they will become. The whole idea and process of experiencing many lives is so that we can learn from each other, learn from the mistakes that everyone will make, and try to atone on the earth for the wrongs that would had been made previously.

The experience of every emotion is a necessity for without this a life cycle would not be complete. It's also important for the return of the spirit back to the homeland. Once they start to evolve back into the realms they can then use their experiences of their earthly incarnations to help and guide people back on the earth. In order to teach you have to have knowledge on the subject. The subject being one of understanding every aspect of living a life in human form, life is never ending. It's full of experiences for us all to learn. We have a lifetime of learning; it never stops until we reach the eternal divine light.

Coming next:

Chapter Six is an introduction to the world of spirit. What's it like living without a physical body? What's it like living where time is beyond measure? What does the spirit world look like?

Six

The Spirit World

Our world can be described in two words, LOVE and PEACE. We surround the earth's atmosphere in transparent energy form. We touch the earth's atmosphere and radiate outwards thus creating the seven realms of spirit. Within each realm there are seven levels with spheres and planes. When the earthly, physical body no longer functions the spirit joins us back in the homeland. The returning spirit will touch the very first level, upon doing this they will be taking their first step back towards the divine light.

If you were to sit in a very quiet darkened room and close your eyes for a short period then open them, you will experience a soft blackness. Imagine within that blackness there are faint whisperings. The feeling around you is one of security, love and peace. Expand your mind to the feeling of tranquillity where all around you is serene. It's a feeling like you have never experienced before. There is no one or anything around you that can cause harm or distress. All you are experiencing is love in the purest form and peace that makes your body feel as if you are floating. There within your mind's eye is the sky of the bluest blue, the yellow of the sun, the green of the grass, the dancing of the flowers and the swaying of the trees.

Then a magical moment comes where you can see the loved ones that you've missed so much spreading happiness and love all around you. You have taken your first glimpse into the homeland. This has all been achieved in your mind's eye with the power of thought driven by the energy which you are creating. Your mind projects the images you expect to see of what you call heaven.

This is our world, a world where we exist by energy and thought. The main aim is for each and every spirit to experience many different processes within each level. Rest then atonement is the first stage for every spirit to go through. From then on there are many avenues which are opened up for the spirit to learn. There is much knowledge gained within the halls of learning and eventually filters back to your earth. This process can take in thousands of years in your earth time. We have no concept of time. Time is irrelevant to us. We are not in a rush.

When a person returns home their spirit stays very much near the earth's atmosphere in order to be able to communicate with the loved ones they have left behind. On your earth time is all important. On earth it could take over seventy years before a spirit starts to evolve. From there they embark upon their chosen pathway. Many of them choose to become guides or become teachers to concentrate on the philosophy side of our world. This is a subject where we have only just touched the surface, a small glimpse for you to understand our world. Once the spirit has experienced all

*levels then it is time to join the divine light. They become as
one with the divine spirit in the purest form.*

We agree with spirit that they have only just touched the
surface of this subject. This is because our working
relationship with the group of eight is based upon them
giving us the information at an introductory level. Picture
the planet earth as seen from outer space. Then superimpose
seven circles or spheres each of a different colour with the
earth at the centre. These seven circles represent the seven
realms of spirit, within each realm there are seven levels of
development. Spirit put it like this:

*"We touch the earth's atmosphere and radiate outwards thus
creating the seven realms of spirit. Within each realm there
are spheres and planes."*

When we return to spirit we will enter the first of the seven
spiritual realms. We will be on the first rung of our journey
of continual growth and development. Over volumes of
time we will progress through the denser energies of the
early realms through to the lightest energy of all in the
seventh realm where we become pure spirit and as one with
God, hence the phrase 'Seventh Heaven'.

Each spirit will follow multiple pathways to growth. These
pathways could involve undertaking repeated incarnations
for instance, to train as a spirit guide to one day become
responsible for a medium on earth, or to undergo extensive
courses in the halls of learning on every subject under the
sun, or train to become a teaching guide. All these pathways
could take thousands of years of earth time to accomplish.

The preparations for a second Being Spirit book entitled *Life & the Afterlife* are underway. As the title suggests the world of spirit will be its centrepiece where spirit will provide more information on the structure of the spirit world as taught to us by spirit.

Singing Winds a Cherokee Indian is one of Steve's closest guides.

He tells of his learning pathway:

My days are ones of contentment. How can they not be when we are in a world where all is peace and love? It is true we learn and evolve deeper into the ether. We become pupils, we become teachers, we are taught and learn and we learn and teach. We have to absorb volumes of information so we can then transmit them back into your world. This is all done in harmony with peace of mind. It is also done for the reason being to help the development and progression of your world. It is done with love. There is much more to tell in the future.

Here is another letter from heaven from Running Bear:

Very few people understand exactly how our world evolves. They know we are there in the ether or in the atmosphere that surrounds your globe. They know that we are spiritual energy in our minds and thoughts. They also know that when a spirit chooses it has the power to communicate with their loved ones who they have left behind.

Imagine it like being a replica of your earthly life except take away all the fear, heartache, noise, disturbances, negativity, harm, hate and revenge. Replace this with positivity light and love. Only these thoughts will surround you and everyone allowing your life to continue in a way that you would never have thought possible. In this energy of pure love and contentment you will find your way forward. You will be able to choose which path to take on your journey towards the eternal flame of light. This takes time of which we have no conception, it is only on your earth that time is important.

Our lesson to you my friend is for you to explain in your writings of how the parallel worlds work. How the two worlds are replicas of each other, how life is continuous without the physical body and how the spirit experience is the true existence of life in its purest form. And although they have exhausted their own physical existence spirits, in our world they are still very much a part of the continuing lives of those they have left behind. They can still witness their achievements and disappointments allowing their spiritual energy to help them along in their earthly existence.

Running Bear describes the spirit world as a replica of our world. As the power of thought dictates what we see; our imagination would create the visions we would expect. Images inside our minds would recreate a world of our own making to include friends and loved ones, rivers, oceans, mountains, any and all visions of contentment and happiness that flow from your mind. After a period of adjustment you will quickly adapt to living as thought and energy. You will enter a state of being, thinking and imagining.

What's it like living without a physical body? In spirit you are pure energy, pure thought consciousness. This is Running Water's explanation:

The spirit has arrived back in the safe hands of their loved ones or a qualified helper to give the love and peace required. After their time of resting, as mentioned there is no time scale on this, time is for your world, they will start to progress and start their journey.

Imagine you have no body, your eyes are closed and you are floating in the air. All around you is extreme peace and you feel no weight at all. Suddenly you want to walk, to place your feet upon the floor, there is no floor. You are in the air. You put your arms out to help you stand, there is nothing for you to hold onto. You are in nothingness. This is an example to help you understand you would automatically open your eyes and immediately come back to a physical perception of your surroundings in your mind.

The spirit would not feel distressed or alarmed only slightly disorientated at first as to how they can operate this new existence without a body. Through the power of thought they would still be able to walk, talk, run, jump, dance, sing, and continue to 'do' whatever they would have done on the earth. You would just have to think it and it will happen.

You will hear many stories from a departed spirit who would have been paralysed when on the earth saying to their loved ones through a medium that my legs and arms are working perfectly well now. I can straighten my back. I could even turn somersaults if so desired. The blind person would say they can see perfectly clearly now. The deaf person would say they can now hear clearly. The mute person would be able to talk. The imperfections of the physical body have been left behind and they are now operating only with crystal clarity from the power of thought.

As we will continuously mention there is no time scale as to how or long it will take the spirit to adjust to the changes they find themselves, it will just happen.

How do spirits know when a loved one is seeking information from them? As mentioned previously many spirits choose to go into a resting period which can then prevent the communication taking place. It is possible for a medium on earth to say 'I have your loved one here' while they are in this state of rest. That would be the influence of the spirit sending out thoughts of love to those who they have left behind. Once the spirit has rested then they are there in energy, because they are thinking of their loved ones or friends they can 'see' their light, which would be the aura wrapped around the physical being on the earth plane.

For the returning spirit during all this time adjusting to life just as thought and mind they would be reviewing their lifetime through the book of life. If a spirit has done harm when on the earth either physically or mentally, they are held back from moving on until they have understood the implications of their actions have had on another person's life. If a spirit has committed extreme acts of evil they will be banished to a sphere of dense energy where they will be isolated for time beyond measure to atone for their actions.

Every returning spirit has to atone and earn forgiveness. They have to forgive themselves for the harm they had caused to others. They have to seek forgiveness from those they caused harm to. This is why you may hear many mediums when relaying a message to a loved one that the communicator is saying sorry and apologising for the harm and hurt they caused when on the earth. The apology has *to be meant, they cannot be lame words. The words have to come with sincerity and truth.*

This will happen to every spirit in whatever way they acted while on the earth. Every one of us has at one point in their lives has something to apologise for. No one is exempt from upsetting others. Running Water wanted to add these thoughts to the Book of Life:

You can compare it to going down memory lane. At times you wish not to be there, but you can't move on until you have explored every avenue of that particular time. Once lessons have been learned and atoned for then you can move onto the next stage. There is not one single step a person has taken that is left out.

It can be interesting and at the same time upsetting for some spirits to be able to view how they made use of the life that was given to them. How they wasted much of their time on earth worrying about the tomorrows that never came. How they wish they had taken more chances while they were on the earth, and how they wished they had taken other people's sensitivities into more consideration. Everyone on your earth at one point in their lifetime has caused some distress in one way or other to someone else, whether it was done mistakenly or intentionally.

The point of all of this is to gradually cleanse and purify the mind for the development and journey of the spirit. This process has no time attached to how long this will take, time is immeasurable.

Every life that was lived is different, every mind was different. People think differently, they have different views and objectives their spiritual growth and journey will take place when the time is right for that spirit.

Every death is different

Every death of the physical body is different and personal to that particular returning spirit. You have to take into account how a person's life was ended, was it sudden, traumatic, peaceful, brutal, expected or would they have ended their life by their own hand? In whatever way a spirit leaves your earth depends at times as to how long they will remain in a resting period. Some choose to stay rested only for a short period while others stay for a longer period of time there is no order of time it is up to the spirit.

There would be no particular personal reason why a spirit would choose to lay dormant for many years. It is common at times for a person on earth to seek many mediums for information on a particular friend or loved one and to come away disappointed because no contact had been made. Their disappointment would increase over time because they would feel that they had done something wrong. Why had the deceased not made contact just to let them know they are happy?

That my friend is all most people left on your earth need to know, is the deceased happy? We have been instrumental in passing over messages from a long departed spirit for the first time in many years. Afterwards the sitter would be jubilant that at last they had had the confirmation they so desired. There is no reason other than the fact that all mediums work on different levels, with different guides and different energies. It would be impossible for every medium to attract every spirit that had departed from your world.

Spirit takes the initiative to contact us on earth. These are White Cloud's words:

> *There is a saying in your world which is: 'I don't agree with people contacting the dead. They should be left alone it goes against God's will'.*
>
> *We contact you on the earth, not the other way round. The choice is entirely left up to the spirit in our world. It is God's will that happiness is spread throughout the universe whatever form that takes. God is universal, the divine pulsing light of energy in the purest form. His light touches every living soul, he is spirit. Would people deny that is happening?*
>
> *Because of the peaceful surroundings where we are, it makes it easier for the returned spirit to contact those who they have left behind; and to give them an indication that they can make contact with them in spirit using a medium. They can transfer some of their loving energies onto the energy field of the ones on the earth who matter. This will let them know that although they have left the physical, they are still very much aware what is happening and how people are feeling and coping with their loss. We bring peace.*

These extra words were added by White Cloud on why returning spirits keep their identity for those left on earth:

> *When the transition takes place from the earth to the homeland a spirit keeps their personality and identity. It stays with them in order for them to be easily recognised when making communication with the ones they have left behind. As has been explained, once the spirit embarks upon their own personal journey they become unattached to the*

earth's atmosphere and evolve further into the realms, thus embarking upon a pathway of their choosing.

After eons of time, many choose a pathway towards the divine light. This is where that particular spirit would have gone through all the processes involved within our world, which would include the cleansing of their spirit, revisiting the life they had led and thus atoning for any mistakes that they would have made. For these spirits they would be enveloped within the peace and tranquillity and continue to ascend towards the divine light.

Others learn and gain as much knowledge and continue on pathways which would enable them to evolve on a much higher vibration, these spirits often choose to become guides.

It's very common in your world to use labels. They play an important part in determining people's status. For many who reside in your world the more important the label the more important the person would sound and the more that person would expect to feel respected. People need labels they can relate to and understand. If the label given would be out of their radar of understanding then that person would dismiss the whole subject. This can be related to the identity of the numerous guides who are working tirelessly within our world. Many of us have dual personalities as we would have led many incarnations. Because we are very much aware of this trait within the people of your earth, we label ourselves according to how we know we will be acceptable to that person.

People on your earth find it easy to gravitate towards Native American Indians. These were and are peaceful people who are at one with the earth and led life in simplicity. Brothers of the cloth, anyone who would have worked in any *of the numerous religious orders on your earth, these also are peaceful and understanding. Medicine men, doctors, nurses, anyone who would have been in the caring sector, people relate to these because of the care and attention, help and understanding they provide. Oriental personalities are labelled as the wise ones, the clever ones, ones who are good teachers. Shaman and holy men would also be powerful entities, with strength and courage.*

White Cloud, Cherokee Native American Indian

Living and Learning in Spirit – The Halls of Learning

Living in spirit is a process of continual development. We've spoken about the eternal spiritual cycle of life where with each incarnation a spirit adds knowledge with every earthly experience. Once a returning spirit completes the resting and cleansing stage the refreshed mind seeks further learning in preparation to embark on another life on earth or to progress within the realms of spirit. Spirit creates an image of the halls of learning. Of course, this is not a physical building with gleaming spires of a hallowed place of learning on the earth but the vision helps us to imagine a place of infinite magnitude with professors, mentors, scribes, scholars and eager students. It is a source of wisdom. It is a thought bank, a magnificent depositary of universal knowledge beyond our comprehension. This is where a spirit withdraws learning from the thought bank to suit their progression to the divine light. Some spirits have described the halls of learning as the university of heaven.

These words are from the group of eight:

In our world once the spirit has become acclimatised to the surroundings there are many choices to be made. The halls of learning are where many spirits go to embark upon new pathways to gain knowledge to pass and filter to the people on the earth. The main avenue for this is to become a spiritual messenger who is there to help and guide people on your earth. To become a guide is a like career ladder. You start at the first rung then gradually and slowly evolve into the higher realms. Along this road the spirit would have experienced many roles to play. Each of these roles are just as important as the next, be it as one of a helper or one of a main guide. There is no hierarchy in our world, we all are equal.

Black Feathers wished to add this explanation:

The halls of learning, how does it work and what happens? Singing Winds likened the halls of learning as a thought bank, which my friend is exactly what they are. Thoughts and knowledge are stored in huge segments of energy where upon the energy can be transferred to the cells of other spirits allowing them to learn. We will call them cells. You can liken them to pockets within the energy mass. This is where all the information that has been learned over time has been stored. Some of the knowledge has been placed there by our universal friends. The rest has been added by very knowledgeable and wise spirits who have been evolving within our realms for an eternity. The amount of knowledge to be learned and taught is huge. It is never ending and covers every subject in the universe. Students only have to think about a subject and the knowledge will flow.

There are many chambers of study within the halls of learning. One is the hall of scribes that has endless rows of teachers crouched over desks quills in hand completing never ending roles of parchment. Broadly half their energies are directed to the education and development of spirit within their world. Their second purpose is to generate and transfer knowledge from them into the minds of mediums on the earth.

Coming next:

How do earthbound religions relate to pure spirituality? How do Native Americans describe their spirituality? Are their conflicts? Is the world of spirit journey's end for all religions on earth?

Seven

Spirit and Religion

These first comments on humanity and religion are from Black Feathers. Spirit uses modern terms, these are their words not ours. They adapt to use modern language for our eyes and ears. This is a subject close to his heart:

Your world is filled with people. You are there in your millions and each and every person is different in colour, creed and personality. There are many languages, many different cultures, and many different beliefs. You all make up the tapestry of life like a huge jigsaw puzzle some pieces interlocking and other pieces refusing to connect. There is much disharmony from citizens who strive to cause problems throughout mankind. These are but a relative few in numbers however their presence is enormous causing many to suffer anxieties and stress. The wish of most is that one day the people of your world will unite together and live for the rest of their lives in peace and harmony.

Is this an impossibility my friend. I think we can all answer that question without having to put too much thought into it. Sadly the disruptive few will always pull the punches leaving the masses that have a good heart always wishing and hoping for the day when peace will reign.

There is one thing that ties many together whether they are disruptive or peace loving, that my friend is religion. There are many different religious groups throughout your world, they are meant to bring peace and love instead they can be the cause of many of earth's wars and atrocities. They give comfort to those who choose to follow their leader. It's universal that mankind need something to believe in and worship. It's Important for many to be able to cling towards a religion that they feel will spiritually reunite those who have fallen by the wayside, and bring that love and trust back into mankind.

Everybody is entitled to believe and worship the religion that gives them hope, faith and trust. It's a common factor that when a person has strong beliefs in one religion they dismiss others thinking their religion is the only one that matters. Others have a broader perspective and can understand the beliefs of others at the same time embracing their own. They all have their Gods that they believe in and have their own theories has to what happens when a person passes away. Each religion has to be respected every person who practices and obeys the guidelines laid down by the head of their religion is to be respected. Although at times some religious groups will home in on people's weaknesses thus making that person feel guilty for thinking thoughts or stepping outside the line of obedience and blocking any thoughts of other beliefs.

It's often spoken about in your world of the beliefs people have in the different type of religions that adorn your kingdoms. There are many of them to be followed. They have set rules that have been laid down by prophets who would have walked upon the soil of your earth. They have used the power of the spoken word to gain many followers. They may have used guilt and they may have used and abused the good nature of many in order to entice them through the doors of their sacred places.

This is sometimes done in good faith. The leaders who have followed the pioneers will always stick steadfast to the rules of which have been taught to them. That is their way. Over thousands of years these religious beliefs have been followed with minor adjustments being made with time as people change with the times. There is one thing that has stayed the same and that is the power of which these leaders can transmit their belief systems into the minds of their followers. Believers have been cajoled into thinking that their religion is for them simply because it was the religion of their forefathers.

It's only natural for parents to take their offspring along to their chosen sacred place. If you have devoted your time to follow the principles of a certain religion it is natural that you wish to pass these beliefs on. Mentoring a person into being a good advocate for any religious beliefs is not wrong, especially if the person or child is willing and understands the scriptures and the guidelines and rules that have been set down before them. It all helps to make the person into a decent human being that will follow and obey the rules of mankind which is to love one another, love yourself, be kind to each other and be kind to yourself. Also to never judge others or yourself, respect others and respect yourself, be human. Use that spirit which is within you to the full potential of your capabilities. Do not be afraid to be yourself. Honesty is not a fault it is a virtue that should be used frequently. People can easily get caught up in the harsh realities of life and all the good thoughts and deeds that are within you can easily be washed away.

If people are forced into following a group against their better judgement then this is wrong for many reasons. It should be the choice of the person if they want to believe in a certain faith, being forced into something that is outside your comfort zone can lead to many complications within themselves. It can cause them to have distorted views or cause much anguish within their hearts can lead to disturbances within their own minds.

It's important for people upon your earth to believe or follow a faith. Through all the centuries that have gone before you people have always sought out a faith that is compatible to them. The point my friend of this conversation is this. In all the different faiths people have followed upon your earth how many of the followers understand who and why they are following that particular faith? They might believe the guidelines and scriptures that have been laid down before them, they might believe in the principles of that faith, the question is do they really understand?

We respect every one of the religious beliefs that are formed within your earth. We would never disrespect any leader or follower. This would be wrong because eventually when their souls leave their earthly body this is where they are welcomed with the pure love from our world and are greeted with the open arms of spiritual warmth. They all return to us in spirit, to our world. When they pass they come to us.

We would never force anyone to become a follower of our world against their own will. It's true we can use our energies to guide and are there ready when a person is willing to join our team but we would never force anyone or fill their minds with guilt or fear. We are not about gaining as many followers or believers as we can. All we want is that people understand our world, understand that life is continuous and never to be afraid of returning back to the homeland.

Allow your mind to choose where you wish to follow. We only want people to understand our world and it to be their choice if they use their skills and gifts which have been given to them. If they feel uncomfortable or inhibited about any of our beliefs we would never force them, we only want to be understood.

Ultimately, all religions worship the same God, the same divine light. The group of guides reinforced the words of Black Feathers in this separate message:

The majority of people that live within your world have their own choices, their own thoughts and pathways to choose. It gives great comfort for many to embark upon a road that will give them comfort, peace and understanding. They fulfil this desire by joining one of many religions on the earth. It is a necessity for many to be able to pray to their chosen God in the hope that one day man will be able to live in peace and harmony. The comfort that can be gained from these religions can be enormous and there are many who join these groups thus sacrificing their lives into helping others by spreading the word of their God.

Each religion is to be respected. Each one gives their followers hope, understanding and a purpose to walk forward in a world that many feel is being destroyed by their fellow man. Whatever belief system a person follows you are still spirit in a human form. When life on earth has ended, their spirit will still come back to the homeland.

When they return their beliefs are still there with them. They are not taken away from them. The choice is there for that spirit to communicate with the loved ones they have left behind if they choose. There is not one person on the earth who could bring forth an unwilling spirit for communication. Each communication that is made is entirely the choice of the deceased spirit. In our world we give great respect to those who follow other beliefs, it is everyone's right to do what they feel is best for them. We do not judge.

The thread that links these teachings is respect for religions which create a code of living in peace and harmony. Followers of one religion should show respect to other religions. Spirit is the ultimate destination for followers of all earthbound religions. When followers pass into spirit they will have their answers.

Black Feathers explained the spiritual worship of Native Americans on earth:

We took pride in our tribes and traditions. Our beliefs were sacred just like people worshipping a god or idol on your earth now. We followed traditions that would have been handed down from generation to generation. We worshipped no idol. Our beliefs were for the earth that surrounded us, the elements, the sun and the moon the animals that were precious to us for they kept us alive through nourishment and warmth.

We would have carved icons, totems, from the wood of the trees. These icons would have had many meanings from the spirit of the earth and not from any prophet who would have lived before us. There would have been many ceremonies just like any religious group except we were not religious inasmuch that we would not have followed a previously incarnated human spirit. Our religion was the earth itself. The people within our territory, our families were of importance to us the children were the future. It was through them that our traditions have been passed on and valued even now in your time.

Spirit is greatly concerned about our planet. This was written by Blue Flame:

Your world the planet of which you all dwell has many wonderful sights, you have oceans, mountains, forests, deserts, frozen ice all of these are precious to the earth's atmosphere. This has been given freely to all who live on the earth. Animals roam freely and there is an abundance of life in the oceans. Slowly and deliberately mankind are guilty of destroying all this beauty that surrounds you. The ice is melting, the forests are being stripped of the trees, and marine life is being destroyed by debris and poison spilling into the oceans. Animals are being destroyed by man for personal pleasure or greed. Gradually the time will come when action has to be taken. Will it be too late? Again the answer to this can only come from your earth, from the people who dwell within it, they need to unite together and stop these atrocities from happening.

The role to protect this beautiful planet is a fundamental duty of human spirits. It is one of the reasons you are here; to use your love and energy to look after Mother Earth.

Before we leave this chapter Five Arrows sent us this message about the stresses and strains of our modern world and the hope that one day people will lead a more spiritual way of life:

The world is filled up with people rushing here and there and getting nowhere fast. They put themselves under much strain and are pressurised by the fast moving energies of which they are creating. This allows them to fall under the spell of disharmony and disorganization. The stress builds up and up until they feel fatigued. All this has a knock on effect to those who are around them. Life becomes a game of skittles where everyone is bumping into one another and knocking each other over. They become impatient, angry, insolent, argumentative, unhappy, all this eventually accumulates into a dense mass of negative energy where it can spread and spread to all those around. My friend if only they knew. Those I have just spoken of are mainly from the developed part of your earth. There are others who reside in parts of your world where modern life has no part. These people live a more genteel existence, living how they would have many hundreds of years ago. Left alone these people go from day to day just caring for others in their tribes and using the art of survival. It's true my friend they will have squabbles amongst themselves and they have their own solutions. The stress of a fast moving world would not intervene within their daily lives. People in your modern world would label them backwards because they have not moved forward and progressed along with the rest of mankind. They would be wrong to think along those lines. These people who reside within these tribes have deliberately chosen to stay and live that type of life. They are at one with the earth and nature. They have not become slaves to your modern society. Their gods and idols would be the spirits of the earth and the sky. They believe and know that there is a force out there helping to give them a stress free and peaceful existence. They believe in everlasting life. These are the two sides of your earth, opposites of one another, one is more balanced then the other except one far outweighs the other causing much disharmony throughout your whole world.

My friend I have made my point for today, Five Arrows

Coming next:

Love and loss are partners in life. How can we come to terms with the loss of a loved one? How can we attempt to fill the void? How can we move on?

Eight

Coping with Grief

Grief is the price you pay for love. The raw, overwhelming emotion of losing someone you love is impossible to capture in words. At first, the void of loneliness is all consuming. Coming to terms with loss can be slightly eased by thinking about them and talking to them. The feeling of loss can be softened by the memories of having them in your life. The times you shared. The joy, the love, and the way they helped you become the person you are today. Those memories will never be lost. They are still with you and will always be with you in spirit. They still care and are looking after you, don't doubt it.

These words from Red Arrow are a comfort from another realm:

There comes a time in everyone's life when they have to experience the true emotions of grief. This is an emotion that affects everyone in different ways. It can be raw like an opened wound it can be like a dull ache that is continuous.

It can be like a pain in the heart causing stress and anguish. However it affects a person you all have that one thing in common which is how long will this pain last? Will it be forever? There is no real answer to this because everyone has to deal with their own personal feelings in their own way.

Grief isn't only just about losing a person back to the homeland people can grieve for many different reasons. It's mainly for the loss of something that was held dear to that person. These emotions are part of the soul for the person to experience life in all stages, whether it is the height of happiness or the depth of despair they are there. How they are dealt with is significant to how you will cope in the long term. For many it's like a path that eventually widens out into a clearing leading onto different pathways allowing space within your inner being to walk forwards into a new beginning. For when you have experienced loss of any kind it is one final chapter closing in your life; therefore a new chapter is ready to be opened and started anew.

Difficult situations in a person's life can be a challenge and to overcome these challenges inner strength and courage are vital threads to be drawn upon. It is not always easy to stand up against an emotion that is strong such as losing someone who has been an important figure in your life. The future in front of you can seem bleak but the dark clouds will eventually fade with time. There is no time limit on this it is different for each individual. Memories play an important part in handling loss they can bring back the happiness you once would have shared together. They can also cause sadness, but whatever feelings they invoke it is the healing process you have to experience to move on and remember that person with the love that surrounds them. They only leave you in their physical form they are always with you with their spiritual self.

Recovering from the loss other than that of losing a loved one also brings challenges of which need strength to recover from. The feelings and emotions are similar in many ways and are just as difficult to cope with. The difference being is that people around you react differently to your circumstances sometimes making the adjustments to your surroundings much more difficult. When on the earth you rely strongly on the support of others around you it's important to have that human support there to help and give the strength of which is needed. People can be very fickle at times and can lose the ability to send their thoughts of help to those who need it; whether it's for the loss of a soul or the loss of something else, but whatever the loss, it is time that will eventually help you recover and move on towards a new beginning.

Life on your earth can at times be very difficult. Challenges are there for you to recover from and how this is handled is different from person to person, your emotions are you. They make you the person who you are. Spirit can help but the strength is there within everyone. It's how you make use of it. It is your own personal pathway one of which has to be led by yourself. Mistakes are there to be made and mistakes are there to be learnt from. Your inner soul is your spiritual self and once a person recognises this then all can be conquered.

The Sadness of Suicide

This is such a delicate subject. Sadly it's difficult to find anyone who has not been directly or indirectly affected by suicide. Spirit wanted us to speak about it with two aims.

One is to bring comfort to those who are reeling from the traumatic loss. The second is for those left behind to know that their loved one will receive understanding in the spirit world.

When someone returns to spirit in these circumstances, they are not punished in the way some earthly religions threaten. They are not banished or turned away from the divine light. They do have to atone for their actions and witness the pain and reactions of those who are still living. All human spirits at the end of their time on earth go through the cleansing process that involves a review of their lives. It is the same for those by their own hand have cut their lives short. Their lifetime is reviewed and their passing is put in context. All the circumstances and emotional situations come into play; not just the traumatic ending. The love and consideration of spirit remains constant for everyone. Traumatic experiences are not exempt from the learning cycle.

The cleansing process for those who have taken their own lives includes working with other departed spirits who took the same early exit decision. Together they will direct their energies to transmit love to their friends and relatives and to anyone on the earth plane who is suffering the pain of such a loss.

The suffering victims on earth feel can last for decades especially if they blame themselves and take the guilt upon themselves. We ask ourselves: 'What could I have done? Was I responsible?' The truth is whether the action was planned or on the spur of the moment, it was carried out by one person alone. It was the end of their current timeline. It was their time to go, as unimaginable as that may seem. Spirit wants survivors on earth to forgive themselves for an act that was out of their control. Spirit does not want you to endure a lifetime of sadness for a decision made by someone else.

A dark shadow is cast on your life. To dispel the shadow we have to realise that no good will flow from living in a miserable state of distress. We have to stop the acid of guilt eating at our hearts and minds. The moment we say 'enough' is the moment when we can make the most of this life; to slowly move forward and live life without the chain weight of sorrow.

There is nothing more certain than your loved one will want you to stop punishing yourself. By punishing yourself you continue to punish them in spirit. Why? Because they feel the pain you feel. Your anger and heartbreak cripples them. Move into the light, do this in love and in their name. Do this so you can both move forward. Life is precious. From personal experience, the emotional fallout lessens to be replaced by memories of happier times.

These words of understanding from Running Water relate to childhood issues leading to adult calamities:

When life is given it is a gift. The individual spirit has chosen to go back to your earth to experience once again the emotions you can only feel when the spirit is within a physical form. Every new spirit chooses an entirely different lifestyle then they would have had in a previous incarnation. They have forgotten the ups and downs life can bring. They have forgotten the heartaches that can occur. They have forgotten that rawness that can penetrate deep within their emotional psyche. Their only thoughts as they grow and mature are how to cope with everyday living. During this new life on earth the child is mainly interested in the world that is closely wrapped around them. If they have the security of a happy and loving family then that becomes all-consuming to them and they can be shielded from all the harshness of the world outside.

The child who has been unfortunate to grow within a sea of upsets and neglect can develop a shield around them to protect themselves from harm. They become a victim of other people's hardships and anxieties causing many problems for their future growth.

Children grow into adults and often their upbringing, surroundings and certain trials they have had to endure can pave the way as to how they will cope with adult life. There are many trials for people to overcome, many difficulties for them to face and conquer, some of these are won and some are lost, it is a testing time.

Everyone has their own individual personality, sensitivities, goals, stamina and zest for life. Everyone has different thoughts, different values and different goals to focus on. Some can conquer all of life's hurdles. Some just cope and there are others who feel they are failures; a failure to themselves and to the loved ones around them. There is no particular type of upbringing that is the cause for anyone to end their own life. It is the choice of the person. It can be a rash decision taken on impulse. It can be thoughts that have been harboured within that person for a long time, torturing their minds in a way where they can become bewildered as to what action to take. Some merely see it as a way out of a difficult situation. It is said that it is a sin to end your life before your time is complete. My friend this is debatable as there are many different mental and physical circumstances to be considered. *However as it has been mentioned life is a precious gift.*

People cling onto life for fear of the unknown. They cling for the sake of their loved ones. Most people wish to live to an old age, they have garnered the thoughts within their minds that is it the natural order of life. Life is precious to most. When a person has taken it upon themselves to end their life by their own hand; many feel anger and shame when so many people are clinging on with hope when their own lives are at risk through illness, starvation or the difficulties of just surviving.

Coming next:

In films you must have seen bogus preachers miraculously healing the sick with the laying on of hands. Is there any truth in it? Can spiritual healing really make a difference and if so how?

Nine

Spiritual Healing

Spiritual healing is the transfer of energy from the universe. A medium acts as the conduit to channel the magnetic power of spirit for the benefit of a recipient. In your mind's eye you could visualise it as a beam of light being directed to soothe, relax and rebalance the body, mind and spirit. Spiritual healing complements, and is not an alternative to conventional medicine. The two modes of healing often work together by the de-stressing and comforting effect of spirit aiding the medical advice and recovery process. The body is relaxed, tensions are eased and self-healing is stimulated.

The ability to provide healing is one of the greatest gifts for a medium. A medium has first to connect with their guide to become a channel of healing. The healing energy is directed from spirit and flows through the medium's palms. Often there's a feeling of heat that radiates, but if the person is angry or stressed the sensation can be reversed to have a cooling effect. This can soothe agitation and anxiety to effectively cool things down. Spirit directs warm, cold or very cold energy; whichever is appropriate.

There are various forms of spiritual healing. The one that people bring to mind most is contact healing where the medium physically places their hands onto someone's body. Another method is for the healer to place their hands near to the body, hovering close but not touching. Distant healing can be achieved by a medium sending healing energy to someone who is close by. Healing can be projected by thought from the medium without the patient being present. This is called absent healing where an experienced healer can attune their thoughts to transfer energy to someone in need wherever they may be.

The hands-on healing process can begin with hands cupped above the top of the head in the position of the crown chakra. To treat the upper body in a sitting position, the medium's hands would move from the top of the head to the base of the back of the neck and rest for a time to let the heat penetrate and provide warmth. The next position would entail the right hand being placed in the centre of the back below the shoulder blades with the left hand either touching or hovering above the shoulder this would concern the heart area.

The downward movement would continue to the lower back with splayed palms. Cupped hands move slowly down each arm to ease aches and pains. Negative energy from the body can be dispelled by the medium seemingly to catch the negative energies in the palms of their hands and dispel them away from the sitter and into the ether. Spiritual mediums can be trained to develop their healing skills. Depending on which healing association they've received guidance from the placement of healing hands differs. One association recommends placing hands on the head, shoulders and back. Another allows healers to move their hands around the body from tip to toe. Spiritual mediums do not have exclusivity for complementary healing. There are other forms of alternative medicine that bring relief.

There are strict codes of conduct involved with spiritual healing. The medium cannot promise to cure a medical condition. They must explain the technique they are going to use and gain permission from the sitter to continue. You should expect the medium to ask whether you have had spiritual healing in the past and if you're currently feeling any physical discomfort or pain. Some mediums will sense pain in another person without asking. Often healing from spirit helps to calm mental turmoil or soothe anxieties. Mediums should not attempt to heal if they are feeling ill themselves as their energy would be compromised. The session lasts as long as needed.

The medium will explain that they will gently tap or pat you on the shoulder when the session has ended. A few moments of quiet will follow as healing can create a serenely relaxed state of mind that should not be shattered by an abrupt end to the session.

White Bear is a venerated healing guide. These are his words from spirit:

The power of healing can be given through many different avenues. The most common form of healing is the laying on of hands or touching the aura or energy field. Absent healing and distant healing are both just as affective in a way although most feel the benefit more from the healer being present.

Healing can also be given by the listening ear. Some people feel they would rather talk to someone who will listen to them. It is a caring therapy to be able to talk to someone knowing that they are listening and not interrupting. Another method can be by just sitting with someone holding their hand in the silence. Words are not always needed they can be disruptive at times.

When healing is taking place the healer becomes a conduit for spiritual energy. The energy from the guide is then transferred to the healer's energy which in turn is transmitted onto the energy field of the person or animal who is receiving the healing. How much strength is in the energy varies from healer to healer. You also have to take into account the physical or mental condition of the sitter.

Spiritual healing is not a cure for all ills. It has never been claimed that spirit can completely heal all illnesses or diseases. It is used for comfort and the relief of many distresses which are caused by illness or one of the many problems people face in their lifetime. You can compare it as a non-invasive therapy which can calm the mind and give spiritual comfort.

There have been many stories in your world where people have claimed to have received healing to find they have been cleared of illnesses where they thought there was no cure. These my friend have been coincidental occurrences. The body at times can cure itself but the healing energy would certainly have helped by relieving stress around that person.

Never forget that a simple word, a smile, an unexpected act of kindness, or just taking the time to listen are all potent forms of healing. This expression of humanity is a potent healing tonic. Purely by being more observant to others and willing to extend a helping hand will produce a warming glow to the person you are helping but you'll feel the warmth bouncing back to you.

We frequently make immediate judgements that are viewed through our own prism. We react quickly without giving thought to the situation or circumstances of the person we are encountering. This is what spirit says on this point:

When you come across strangers in your daily lives it's a human trait to make split-second judgements as to how that person is presenting themselves. People are oblivious to the circumstances in their lives as to why strangers are appearing in a certain manner. That person may have received bad news or are experiencing unhappiness, a smile and a kind word can lift their spirits a little and help them get through their day. People should learn how not to make rash judgements about each other until they have all the knowledge and facts.

We would like it to be as it is in our world where to be judgmental is unheard of. Alas my friend, people on earth will only realise this when they return to the homeland. If people in your world were to give a lot more thought to others around them then maybe the negative energies which flow around many people would fade to a very fine mist, allowing each other to breathe more easily and start to understand each other in a way where more positivity is in place.

A smile can be like sunshine to someone who is experiencing a dark cloud above their head. A handshake can be like a velvet glove bringing warmth from the cold. A gentle hug can be like an angel bringing the light from the dark. To give someone a few minutes of your time can be like receiving a gift from heaven. My friend if you all look out for each other, strangers as well as friends and family, then gradually your world might become easier to live in.

These words from spirit describe the healing directly generated from their world:

It's common in our world to give healing to the relatives and friends of the deceased. This helps them come to terms with what has happened in their lives. This is done by the thought process of the working spirits many of whom are angels. They are known in our world as the Sisters of Mercy. It is their main purpose to care for children and people who have passed into spirit in traumatic circumstances. This is done by transmitting the pure light and love from the realms of our world. Healing helps in a subtle way. Healing energy is like a cloak that is wrapped around the body's aura or energy field. It is love from spirit that eventually filters through to the inner self gradually helping the person to cope with their grief or stress.

This healing process is also used for many other reasons that interrupt the daily lives of the people on your earth. It is the pure white light and love of spirit filtered from our energy to your energy to help heal the soul.

When a person on the earth is suffering from an illness, it's common for that person to expect that the healing will cure all ills, even if the illness is terminal. It's unfortunate that the healing powers cannot cure all ills. It's administered in order for the sufferer to feel calmer and less stressed and is able to cope with their lot.

As I was adding this last transcript a tragic event was happening in the real world. Love and understanding were nowhere to be seen:

LONDON TERRORIST ATTACK – 22nd March 2017

A terrorist drove a vehicle onto the pavement running along Westminster Bridge, then crashed the car into a gate by the Houses of Parliament. The attacker then stabbed and killed an unarmed police officer, Police Constable Keith Palmer. Four pedestrians died on the bridge. These were Aysha Frade, Kurt Cochran, Leslie Rhodes and Andrea Cristea. As you read their names send healing rays to their loved ones and to the victims now in spirit. Forty other people were injured in the incident, some critically. The attacker will atone for his actions in the next world:

This message was received by Janet at 20.53hrs on the same evening of the attack:

Your world is and will never be in complete harmony. Throughout the ages there always have been wars and disputes that have shattered lives and dreams of many who have lived a life on your earth, and so it continues and will always continue. The human spirit is a divine light that is put upon the earth in the purest form. When the spirit takes its first breath once it hits the earth's atmosphere that is when the spirit within that baby new born is put to the test.

In our world we receive every second of your earth's time questions from the people who reside on earth, the one main question is WHY?

It is such a small word with an enormous impact.

When a spirit chooses the right to a life the choice is given to them as to which pathway they would like to experience. No spirit chooses to be evil, no spirit chooses to kill or maim innocent people. No spirit chooses to hurt those who they love. Those choices are made within the human mind when they start their life's journey. It's an accumulation of many of life's rituals that can interfere with the way their minds are working, the choices of right and wrong are within everyone to understand.

They are within your emotions. They are there to help guide you along the way. The majority of people living within your earth abide by these rules. It's common for people to stray a little away from these rules. Every person on earth at one time in their lives has been guilty of causing distress or slight harm to another but a stronger emotion, guilt. Guilt is there to help that person understand their actions and hopefully make amends to the injured party. They have to learn within themselves that you have to earn forgiveness. If you can't forgive and love others, how can you expect to be forgiven and loved?

There are also people who through no fault of their own have an unsound mind; this is an illness. These people need love and protection from the many evils that can be attracted to them. They need guidance and with the correct care and attention. They are taught the rights and wrongs and an understanding that you each have your own choices to make and to respect your fellow man. Those who step away from the rights and wrongs and respect for others act upon their own thought process of what they think in their minds is the correct way. Some act out of sheer impulse that they immediately regret. Others feel guilt after the deed has been done, and there is no going back for that person. Some take it upon themselves to carry out more senseless acts of violence without feeling remorse.

They are not being guided by spirits good or bad. They are acting entirely on their own commands. Some like power. Power is addictive. Power is the cause of most of life's atrocities. Power can be like a tumour that grows and distorts a person's mind into thinking that they can be invincible. So, therefore, they are acting upon their own thoughts.

Each and every person who resides on your earth has to make choices in their lives. Spirit is not responsible if the choices they make are the wrong ones. Spirit can guide, but if it is the choice of that person to ignore any good thoughts that are being filtered through to them then there is nothing spirit can do. It is up to each person to live with their conscience.

When such people, who act without conscience and cause atrocities, harm and distress, come back to our world, their spirit is sent to another realm where it would be impossible for them to blend in with other energies. They have to learn to atone for their behaviour and are not given the opportunity to make contact with people who they have left behind.

The reason why that is done is to send and spread love from our world to yours. This would be impossible for that to happen to someone committing such a horrendous act. Because if you have not acted out of love and respect for others then you would have no right to expect to return to the homeland to be enveloped in warmth and love. It wouldn't be right for that criminal to expect to return love until they have earned that right. It is a process that will take that person a very long time. There is no spirit that can evolve towards the eternal divine light until they are completely cleansed and purified.

Life is given to you. Life is a precious gift. Life is to take responsibility for your own actions and not to blame others for any bad decisions. Spirit is life. Life is eternal and you each have to atone for your mistakes when you return to the homeland. Make those mistakes as small as possible. Spirit forgives. But, you have to forgive yourself as well.

Coming next:

Getting to know the spirit guides as people has been a joy for us. Each one has a distinctive character and a compelling human story from their time on earth. Get ready to meet the group of eight and the members of Running Water's circle too.

Ten

Meet the Guides

We'd like to dedicate this penultimate chapter with our greatest thanks to the spirit guides within the group of eight and the members of Running Water's circle in spirit. In their own words, this is how of the Group would like to be introduced:

To the reader: Our group has been formed in our world for many decades. We are made up of eight guides, all of whom have been working together for the sole reason to help guide and teach those people on your earth that choose to work alongside us in the capacity of a spiritual medium. For the newly developing mediums there are guides who are taught by us to lead them on their new journey. These would be trained guides who reside on a lower level, they are still being trained by us while they are training and working with the developing medium.

On this journey we have communicated through thought. Our words are transmitted to the mind of this medium who in turn will deliver it to the writer. These mediums were chosen by us for this work for their combined energies and strength. It is a journey that will lead them further on their spiritual pathway.

We all have our different roles to play. We all have different personalities. Each one of us is here for a reason. There is the one guide with patience, one who is impulsive, one who likes to be the mediator, one who likes to have hearty discussions, one who will push hard, one who has an open mind, and one who will disagree. Then there is the leader, the overseer of all, the wise one whom we all look up to, yet we are all equal. This group is a fine balance of energies that have chosen to work together in order for us to pass on our knowledge.

We work with many mediums on your earth and we work differently with every medium we choose according to their abilities. These two mediums we have chosen for a project to explain about our world in simple terms, a project where it would get the interest of many who otherwise would dismiss us. It is a platform for people to work upon. If you wish to explore more of our world there would be more knowledge and literature available which would be able to widen your mind and interest, we wish you all well on your journey.

Introducing individual members of the Group:

The Group have gathered once again and we feel it is about time we made our introductions.

It's been spoken to you that the head of our group is someone famous in your world. We would like to take this opportunity to explain about this great leader. He resides and takes the head of many groups in our world. He is not the highest spirit in our existence he still has many levels to conquer. His name is Tatanka Iyotake of the Hunkpapa Lakota. My friend you would be aware that highest status goes to the divine light, the infinite being. We do not have labels in our world as to who is better than anyone else. It's merely explaining the order of longevity and development back in our world.

He is a very wise master and has gathered much valuable knowledge which in turn he teaches to his pupils. These are other spirits evolving towards the eternal light and along the way wish to gain as much knowledge as possible in order to filter this back to your earth. It is the knowledge from our world that helps people in your world progress and for them to make changes for the future. Imagine on your earth a professor of infinite knowledge. He takes great pleasure in sharing that knowledge with anyone who is eager to listen and learn. He will teach groups of great advancement, also groups going back down the scale to beginners. There is no-one who he will not help.

Our group consists of guides of a high grade who have had to gain much knowledge from hard work. It might be added that it is a joy and privilege. In our world only peace and love exist; everything we learn is carried out with pure love and clarity.

He has many helpers who work alongside him who also in turn head certain groups of their own. Each group undertake many different subjects, some of which differ greatly from one group to the next, but whatever the subject it is equally important as another.

To the right side of our leader sits Blue Flame, Five Arrows, Black Feathers, Red Arrow, Rain Cloud, Brown Bear *and Morning Mist who will be on the left hand side, thus securing the circle. Running Water, White Cloud, Wang Chang and White Bear are guests of this group and are invited to sit amongst us. Behind us will be our helpers which Singing Winds would be one of them and not forgetting Wang Chang's twelve scholars. There are others too numerous to mention but equally important.*

This message is from Singing Winds who wishes to pass on this knowledge from the leader of the group. The tipi has been assembled with the members of the group. The head of the group, Tatanka, wishes to extend his blessings to you and to tell you more of his life on earth:

My dear friend when I was on the earth living my life I encountered many misfortunes. We were living a peaceful existence for a short time until the white man came and decided that everything they saw and touched belonged to them. They were blinded by anything that was new to them. They saw our people and our way of life an intrusion into their way of life. It was never in their intelligence to join us and be interested in our ways and learn from us. All they wanted was to take from us and for us to fall into to their way of living.

We were of the land they stole from us claiming they had the right to take away everything that we worshipped and valued. They said it was the 'new world' and they had a right to make claims upon it. It was our heritage. Our forefathers worked hard to instil pride into each and every one of us. The white man called us savages because we were talking in our mother tongue. They forget my friend it was they who were the invaders. They ridiculed our rituals which we had been performing for hundreds of years claiming we were backward and was forced to learn the white man way.

We retaliated and fought against the injustice that was being put upon us. I stood tall and held my ground for the love of my people and the land that we grew to love. I was always true to my word. We were proud people. I fought and won battles and later I even joined their side to prove that we could all live and work besides each other in good faith. My reward came in the form of betrayal from the people I came to trust.

That was in my time. Since that time many moons ago people say they have learned from past mistakes and want to learn about our ways and rituals. Many of us have become famous names upon your earth. We are now looked up to instead of being looked down upon. We are worshipped and treasured. The lands we fought so hard to keep for our homes belong to no one. They belong to the earth. Our spirits and memories are embedded upon the soil that took so many lives protecting it.

My friend I came to spirit harbouring no ill will. I forgave those who betrayed me and my people. From then on every spirit that has joined me in my world has had to learn how to forgive themselves for the atrocities they would have committed on your earth. They have had to sift through every emotion they possess and learn from all the mistakes they made. Even I would have had to go through the same process.

To forgive those who have done ill towards you means you can walk forward instead of always looking back. Your spirit will grow in strength. You will gain knowledge and wisdom. You will be able to embrace any new knowledge that is to be put before you. You will shine.

My role is to teach in a way where vast knowledge is channelled into the minds of those who are ready to receive. Judgement is not for me or any spirit to place upon anyone. The day of judgement comes my friend for each of us when the physical existence finishes and the spiritual one begins. That is when mankind have to own up to the mistakes they committed when on the earth. The journey to the infinite light can prove to be an enlightening one where the spirit will truly gain a wealth of wisdom.

Singing Winds wanted to add his own account of the tipi the groups meeting place. He describes his entrance after being away from the group for a while. Spirit guides and departed spirits remember themselves as we remember them when they were on earth. This is true for our loved ones who have passed recently as well as those like Singing Winds who passed hundreds of years ago. During the writing of this book the group of eight held 'virtual' meetings in either their tipi or in a formal setting of an auditorium, or spoke to Janet as individuals through channelling. Spirit uses these mental links to help us visualise the proceedings in terms we would understand. As you know there are no solid structures in a world of mind and thought. It is the energy of imagination.

The Tipi: It is quite large. The opening is to the right of you. There is a circle of loose stones in the middle where the fire is. On the floor all around the sides are skins all scattered around. A Buffalo skull, our sacred animal, is in the outer floor of the tipi. Drawings of friends and scenes from our native world hang on the inside of the tipi.

Sitting to my left is Running Bear. He has a fur hat on his head and a short fur coat, he is looking at me and smiling and says 'where have you been, we have been waiting for you for a long time?' I'm a tall Indian warrior, quite slim, rugged skin and of good years. I have scars on my face through battle. I sit down facing Running Bear and make a tribal sign. I would have been killed in battle and my name is Singing Winds.

I was from the Cherokee tribe and of the character was that nothing would stop me in my tracks. If a thought came into my head it would drive me along until my job was done. I was fearless but compassionate, impulsive and quick to judge. This was a trait that had to be refined now I am no longer on the earth.

There is to be a meeting. I stay sitting and one at a time others are filing into the tipi and we do a strange hand shake. There is a lot of laughter around, the flap opens and in comes the leader. I know this because there is a lot of respect. He exudes charisma and importance. Running Bear is talking to me in tongues and we laugh then all goes serious. The leader has a long pipe (it's thin, more like a hollow reed rather than a clay pipe we would envision). It is now being passed round. There is complete silence and peace. The meeting begins.

They are talking about past battles for land, they are speaking very quickly. They are pleased that I have joined them now after such a long time. The meeting is now over they all seemed pleased with the way it went. I rise and walk through the flap, outside waiting for me are others on horseback. They are younger than I am, my horse is ready, and I mount. After farewells, and we ride away.

This is how Janet described how the gathering assembles when meetings are held in the auditorium:

It's like they put me in the centre of the arena and I'm looking out towards the audience. I watch all the guides file in. The higher guides take the front seats and the rest all sit behind. The head of the guides always sit on the front row in the middle and they fan out accordingly.

White Cloud sits next to him as he is Steve's guide. Wang Chang sits on the other side and I have Running Water with me in the circle. Running Water has to be with me because he is my guardian and protector. When a question is put to the group it's known that they argue amongst themselves and they can become very vocal. Other spirits arrive to listen and learn from the proceedings.

Introducing White Cloud

This is White Cloud's first message to Steve channelled by Janet:

My friend, I have been with you many years. I have witnessed sadness and distress within your life and the search for peace. It can be hard at times for us as a guide when we have to watch our chosen medium make mistakes, it has to be done, it is life, and it is how people learn. We choose our time when we guide you onto a clearer pathway. It has to be done with your choosing, when you realise the time is right for you to make amends. Your search has taken you along pathways of inquisitiveness and understanding. I have been there all the time leading you from one path to another until we knew the time was right to bring you to your rightful pathway. Many times I remained a silent guide. The time is now right for me to introduce myself to you. My role within the group is one of a guest. My status in my world would be one of the same level as the group. Is it the same level as Running Water who is the main guide for Janet. I am the main guide for you. There are many others which include Singing Winds, as time goes on we will introduce others who are an important part in your spiritual life.

When choosing who we are to follow we choose people of similar character, we have many of the same traits, we choose like for like, this is so our energies can blend to the fine tuning we need for complete harmonisation. My time on earth would have been long in years. My status within my tribe would have been an important one where there were many decisions which would have been placed before me. We would have travelled at times for survival. That would have meant my one aim was to look after and care for others within our fold. Because of this I had to hide my sensitive nature and adopt one of assertiveness and at times arrogance.

I wished for and eventually found peace and contentment. We work together differently than that of Running Water and Janet. It is necessary for the blending of a continuous partnership. The group are and always will play an important part in our journey. I will consult them many times where there will be new turnings in our direction. We are good leaders. We are there in complete friendship and will never lead you on a wrong pathway.

White Cloud, Cherokee Indian

Running Water's Circle of Spirit Guides:

Previously, we described how members of a spiritual circle gather to tune into spirit and develop their psychic skills. You are about to meet members of Running Water's spiritual circle. Each guide has their particular talent that they bring to the circle which together with their own distinctive story has created an inspiring group of 'real life' characters. Through Janet they address me as writer or scribe as the person who records the information:

Running Water:

> I am known to Janet as Running Water. We have been in partnership since she was bought back to this earth. My energies remained silent until the time was right for her to join us on our journey. A journey which has had its ups and downs, happy times and sad times, we are a partnership. Our energies have bonded and blended in a way where trust has been firmly placed between us. We lead, she follows. That is true friendship, believing and trusting. Her journey has only just begun, everything that went before was just a rehearsal until the joining of energies were entwined in order for the main work for spirit to begin. The work now has begun.
>
> I am a Native American Indian who came from the Navaho tribe. We were peaceful people who hunted only for survival. We faced many trials throughout our lives. There was nothing we could not overcome. I had two wives, both of whom I outlived, four sons and three daughters and many grandchildren. My time in Spirit has been spent training and learning. Janet is my first medium for whom I am the sole

protector, her main guide, as I like to say, the one who pulls the spiritual strings. We are a joint partnership.

It is my responsibility to protect her. She works with us for the purpose of channelling. We have spoken many words to many people and have produced much evidence. During this time, it was never my intention to give clairvoyant messages. We in spirit only wanted to talk and answer questions about our world. But it was quickly established that certain people on your earth were more interested in their material life. In order for me to develop with Janet I had to give those clairvoyant messages so that was the path that we had to follow. My friend, for many years we have had many meetings in this way until Tahonka came and joined our circle and it is now him who is working with her with her clairvoyance. She is developing her gift of channelling with me as was originally intended.

Wang Chang

Wang Chang is on a higher level than Running Water. He is a guest of the circle who likes to teach. We are aware you have been acquainted with him, once met, never forgotten. He is from the Ming Dynasty and is a very clever and wise guide. You will have many conversations with him over the years. Wang Chang is his own master. He is an important visitor to my group he will come and go as he wishes and when he feels he is needed. Wang Chang was Running Water's teacher. He is a hard taskmaster. He is also your teacher and will test you with riddles to make sure you have learned your lessons well. Wang Chang smiles and laughs, he has a twinkle in his eye as he introduces himself. He says he is always 101% right. That's because he is.

Canuji

Canuji is the most serious of the guides within the circle. He is very caring and a great healer. Witch Doctor or Medicine Man is used to describe him. He has a team of workers who are healers and like to use old fashion methods of healing. Grasses and herbs are his main instruments. His symbol is of a Black Panther. If you are in pain or ailing in health then you are at liberty to visualise this symbol, he has given you permission. He would have been placed on your earth in the region of East Africa. His journey back to spirit was in his second decade due to an infection from a wound in his arm. He rarely speaks now within the group but is always in attendance.

He is very sensitive in nature and is only interested in the health of any person in the meeting or their animals. He is very sincere in the role he plays and will be a rarity if he ever gives a message. Occasionally he will impart information about the health of someone who isn't present in the meeting. His main interest is to keep people well in mind and body. He is regarded as a prince amongst his people. His costume of the skin of the Black Panther maintains his position amongst his tribe. He is very proud, they were a proud people.

Abdullah

Abdullah would like to introduce himself personally and has been given permission:

Welcome, my friend. It is with great pleasure that my introductions can be directed from me personally. It's never been in my favour to have someone else speak for me. I have always liked to be known as the wise one, the fixer, the one who can sort out problems for another.

When it was my life on the earth my geographical position was in North Africa, the country would be known to you as Egypt. My town has now been long gone, covered in dust and entwined within a city. My trade was that of a merchant in cloth and of many other items that would have been useful for the home. My other main purpose was that of money lender. People would come to me with all manner of problems; be it if their donkey's legs had buckled, or if the wife had committed adultery, or if they had no means to buy food for their children.

There was nothing I could not fix. People would travel for miles and days for my services to help them with their problems. Each night when it was quiet, I would walk into the desert and gaze towards the sky and consult the stars, the celestial beings. That was where my guidance would come from. The stars became my guardians, the whisperers, the helpers of all. I would relay any concerns to the stars and would be rewarded with the correct solution.

It was only when my spirit came back to this world that I realised that all along it was the help from spirit. They served me very well my friend, so it was understood from the beginning that was my pathway, to help your troubled earth. My part within the circle is enjoyable, I like to utter words, and I like to give my opinion. We will meet my friend when the dust has settled and the time is right.

The specialist role Abdullah likes to play within the circle is that of an advisor. The main purpose of his intervention is to give everyone hope that although at the time of hardship there is nothing that cannot be resolved. Every argument or altercation has two sides and it is up to the parties involved to listen to each other with an opened mind. He has a huge sense of humour. The reason he talks of vast distances between his clients and himself is to place in everyone's mind that at times of distress and anger there should be a cooling down period. This gives the mind time to absorb all that has on gone and to be able to come to a mutual decision. It is a subtle approach in advising people to think rationally rather than irrationally.

Charlie

Charlie known as Charles Short nickname Lofty is from London's East End. He lived into his twenties and was taken from this earth in World War II during a bombing raid during the Hitler's Blitz. He likes to tell his own story which will be given to you when you meet him.

He is the most popular of the guides. His great sense of humour relaxes of those who are sitting and maybe feeling nervous. His energies are those of a common person who would have lived on the earth and through life did not achieve a high status of success. He comes across as someone who is funny, cheerful and not too fond of authority. He just likes to talk.

He is and always will be the most popular of the guides who converse because of his ability to give everyone in the meeting a relaxed view of spirit. He is very clever; his cheerful manner disguises how shrewd he is. He can quickly reduce any anxieties and does give meaningful messages although it can seem he hasn't given a message at all.

Jonny Whistle

Jonny Whistle is a cheerful and jolly personality. His main role is to inform people of the suffering people have to endure because of greed. He likes to point out the differences between wealth and poverty, how wealth can distort a person's mind into gluttony. He loves freedom and the feel of the plant life that surrounds him.

His purpose is to remind people to look out for and care for each other. His singing is a reminder to all that although you are going through dark times it does not necessarily mean you have to give in to negativity. Negative thoughts to him bring on illnesses. His one love is to see that people are well fed it's an indication to him they are above the poverty line. His main aim is for people to think about others. Jonny Whistle lived in England in the middle ages. He has a cart pulled by his trusty horse Bobbin and together they ride round the countryside giving healing potions and sharing an abundance of love and laughter.

Friar Saul

For a man of the cloth he was very fallible. His love of ale, cheese and ladies to keep him warm at night led to him being turned out of the monastery in England around the time of Robin Hood. As a spirit guide he has been invited into my group to point out to people on earth the contradictions of life. And to show that people who are giving others advice are the main culprits behind these contradictions. Friar Saul will also comment on how people will gladly blame others to take away the argument from themselves. The point he is making is that the sinner will always place the blame on others. They will always make an excuse for their behaviour. They have no moral standards in their lives; to them they are the only person that matters. Friar Saul is a larger than life character.

Peter

This spirit is very shy, gentle and humble. He has a stutter. In life he would have always been backstage and in the shadows. He lived and worked in his parents' book shop in Victorian England at the time Charles Dickens was writing. His special role is to be able to give a sitter a glimpse back in their life by telling personal stories as if he is reading from a book that has been written only for them. This is his way of giving them the knowledge that through time every episode of their life will fade into the background, and another new path will form. The telling of their lives through a story gives them the feeling that spirit is watching them and looking after them. He will often touch on the vulnerable times in someone's life allowing them to look upon that period in their life with fondness, even though at the time it may have caused them distress. The reason he likes to read his stories out loud as if he was reading from a book is to give the sitter a sense of togetherness with his energy. He is a very wise spirit and will bring much pleasure to the sitters and yourselves.

Josiah

On first impression Josiah is a solitary figure who likes nothing better than to sit in his room and write. Josiah has a very sensitive energy and always needs assurance that all will be well in the world when he is outside of his study. His eyesight is worsening after years of writing by candlelight with his quill on parchment. He loves nothing more than sitting on his veranda in the evening air with his wife Eliza or walking around the garden when he's feeling vexatious to calm him. He wonders at the beauty of nature and the visiting humming birds. He will be very amusing, wishing only to converse rather than give messages. He can go very deep into the mind but at the same time hover above the surface. He only feels comfortable within his own type. He will automatically pick up on anyone in a meeting who is not genuinely interested in our world. Many people think they know all there is to know about the realms. Josiah will always be one step ahead and will not falter from letting them know. Josiah was a member of the Quakers or The Religious Society of Friends. He had a son Ezra and a daughter Ruth. Josiah is a hopeless romantic. Here's a love poem written for his wife Eliza, transcribed by Janet from one of his messages to us:

"How my heart sings when I hear your voice
How my heart sings when I see your smile
You came into my life like an angel falling from heaven
You are my own precious gift.
How I smile when I see you happy
How I am sad when I see you sad
You are mine to love and protect
You are my own precious gift
The colours of the rainbow
Dance around you like sparkling gems
Through the clouds the rays of the sun shine like a torch from

heaven upon your hair
The wind brings colour to your cheeks like apples
You are my own precious gift
You light up my life
You lift up my soul
You fill my heart with love
You were sent to me and I to you
We are our own precious gifts to each other"

Josiah adds:

Eliza would place all my words together tied up with string and placed in a box and when she would be feeling melancholy she would take them out and read them over and over again.

Josiah has asked us to produce a book of his love poems. What do you think?

Moondance

She is Running Water's most precious granddaughter whose role is to stay silent and help relax sensitive people. She tunes into sensitive energies and channels wisdom and courage. We will learn more about her when the time is right for her to take an active role in the circle.

Tahonka:

His role is to channel the messages to Janet. He has worked with her for many years. His identity is yet to be disclosed.

Tahonka is present when Janet when gives clairvoyant messages for sitters in private meetings, with groups or to church congregations. He acts as her gatekeeper to review the messages that individual spirits want to deliver to their loved ones to make sure they are suitable and obey the three golden rules that Tahonka repeats of never giving bad news, never giving personal and sensitive information away in an open session and never to embarrass.

Running Water concludes:

That my friend is our circle. Working mediums in your world are similar to guides in our world. The more you develop and progress you are moved to another level. It is like any form of learning; the more experienced you are, the further you will go. We work with mediums who have gained experience through dedication and perseverance. We often work in the capacity of direct voice, where we would use the medium for channelling. We would be able to speak via the medium using their voice. This way of working can be beneficial to the guide; it is a way of communicating directly from spirit to the people on your earth.

Brother Oliver and Christina known as Sister Theresa, along with Shining Star, Flaming Star, Blue Mountain and Lone Wolf are all welcome visitors to Running Water's circle.

Coming next:

This is our final chapter. Spirit will give their farewells until we meet again in the next Being Spirit book, when more life affirming messages will be channelled for you. In the meantime, the question: 'What are we doing here?' will be answered.

Eleven

This Life

This message was spirit's way of alerting us that Being Spirit Book One was coming to a close:

Everything that needs to be heard has been written. You will shortly be coming to the end of the written word. We have given you our thoughts and you used them in the way which was directed from spirit. The seeds of thought have been put in motion so that you will be guided by us as to what direction you will follow. We are there in your thoughts. Follow the leads which are placed within your mind, there are many outlets open to you and each one will lead you to where you should be.

From the first page Janet and her spirit guides have placed the emphasis on supplying evidence of the existence of the spirit world. This involves guides, angels and all forms of celestial beings, all working as messengers of the divine.

Why are we here?

The answer is simple: To live your life, to embrace your spirituality.

This message from Josiah puts it beautifully:

To love and bring peace upon the earth for everyone is God's desire. He will always be there to love and never judge. His words are: 'Go my little children, live a life on the earth, explore your own identity, learn from each other and learn from yourself. You will come back to me with many questions and apologies of how you failed. No one is a failure. Some find it harder to learn by their own mistakes. It is one of life's lessons of which there are many. You are sent forth with love and you will be received back with love. The journey of life is a lesson in itself'.

It is for you to complete the ultimate experience of living this lifetime on earth. To suffer setbacks and celebrate achievements, to know sadness and elation, to make mistakes and cope with the consequences, to feel pain and anguish and recover, for your heart to burst with unconditional love, to feel anger and vindictiveness and understand that's a challenge to acknowledge and remedy faults and mistakes, to forgive and ask forgiveness, to learn the value of caring for this planet and every aspect of it, every living thing and the environment, to overcome adversity, to show compassion, and finally to know yourself and to have the courage to accept what you find. To grow.

At birth, human spirit is pure. It is the impact of living your life that shapes character and personality. In broad terms it is a combination of those two factors we hear about namely, nature and nurture. Nature is your inherent biological make-up and received through genes and passed on through family bloodlines. This reflects aspects such as height, weight, and vulnerability to illness. The environment, parental influences and formative experiences are elements in the nurturing of someone's character and personality. These factors shape this existence, this time on earth. Your spirit will evolve. Remember the analogy of the sunflower, this lifetime will not be your last.

The Next Step?

Accepting Spirit into your life does not mean questioning any beliefs you already hold. It does mean finding joy and comfort from knowing the divine is inside you. We opened the book with Janet talking to the spirits of loved ones, speaking to them as if they were here in the flesh. Those spirits were once your family or friends or lovers. They breathed this air. They lived with you. They ate at your table. They laughed. They shed tears. They loved. They left when it was their time. They were speaking to Janet from a world away. In the future, you will join them. You will be in spirit connecting with your loved ones back here on earth. The cycle turns. The two worlds combine. Passing from this world starts a different phase of existence. It is not the end. It is the transition to a new beginning.

Take all you've read as life affirming. You now have evidence; evidence on these printed pages that this life does not have a dead end. Sing in the shower, dance to the music, laugh with friends until your ribs ache, travel, live life to the full knowing your loved ones are by your side. Make love, create love, and give love. Know that your spirit guide is your friend and companion. Know that your guardian angel is with you 24/7. Speak to them. Get on with living. Cast off negativity. Live for the moment. Love is the message.

Throughout our time on earth we must learn to be our own person. To know ourselves, to rely on ourselves and become one with the skin we live in. That is not to say we cannot love others or that we must be isolated and alone. We arrive alone and will leave the same way. Lone Wolf touches on this subject so we recognise and take responsibility for our own thoughts and actions. These are Lone Wolf's words on being solitary:

The reason for my communication is on a subject that is not often spoken of; that my friend is solitude.

Would you agree with me my friend that people shun away from conversing on such a subject as this? For is it not thought of in your world as being lonely? You may be a lone warrior in amongst people who gaggle away together not giving much thought as to what is being said or done. Because they are together in a group they are not alone. They feel they are being enclosed with love and protection. They feel united as a group, therefore they feel they belong. Belong to whom?

Step outside the family unit for just a moment. Many people forget they have one mind, a mind which is theirs and belongs to no one else, this mind is you. It is spirit come to live in a human form. Your true mind has forgotten all the rules and knowledge from whence it came. It has been wiped clean for the new life you are to lead. It is your new life on Earth.

Developing in your world is most probably one of the hardest tasks any spirit has to undertake. Your spirit takes human form. This becomes a person with needs, with wants, with decisions and choices to make. Mistakes are made but are they learned by. Sometimes they are ignored or given to someone else to take the blame because the giver refuses to take responsibility for their own misdemeanours. Many people act in this manner because the fear of be rejected, put aside, forgotten, to be alone, to live a life of solitude, never to be part of a group again.

This is nonsense my friend. These fears are for your world, they do not exist in my world which makes it all the harder when the spirit suddenly finds they have to take full responsibility of the life which has been given to them. This is why many feel the need to gravitate towards groups of people living their life, not as they would like but as part of a group. Groups do not consider the needs of the individual. The fear of living freely is something a group member cannot entertain because to them they would be leaving behind the imaginary protective layer the group has created.

My friend to live a life of solitude has been greatly misunderstood. It means to be free, in charge of one's own spirit, to be able to mix and converse with people in a way where you have no worries or misconceptions about yourself. It means to be prepared for the paths ahead, to be able to open and shut doors when the need arises. Solitude means to like and be completely comfortable and peaceful within yourself, and never to be afraid of being alone. You are never alone when you have chosen this pathway because the only person who you have come to rely on is yourself and no one else. It takes strength and courage to get to this level of living, it brings rewards it means you have discovered your own identity.

This does not mean it will be impossible to love and cherish others, on the contrary my friend, a living spirit such as this makes for the most reliable companion and friend anyone can wish for. They have humility, compassion and the understanding that is sometimes needed when a person has problems they do not wish to share but do want support and companionship.

Life is a turnstile my friend. You go in one side and come out the other. Sometimes it can get stuck and refuses to budge, but with patience it will turn smoothly again. Life is the most precious of gifts that can be bestowed upon a person, some cherish it, some abuse it, whichever way you walk through life it's best to understand that is the only life you'll remember. So live it well my friend be true to yourself and others and achieve the goals which are set before you. Live for your own happiness for when you come back to spirit the less regrets a person has, the happier they will be.

Lone Wolf

This is the last word from spirit:

The purpose for us to produce these written words was in the hope that whoever reads this can gain a small amount of understanding about the realms of spirit. It was never our intention to preach or to lure people into our fold. That has to happen willingly.

Over time there have been many books written on every subject involving our world. There is much in-depth information for people on all different levels; every person *has a different level of understanding. The information is there for people to further their inquisitiveness and increase their knowledge. It has to be taken step by step, right from the beginning. If you feel you would like to explore more, the literature and learning will be there.*

We have touched on various subjects very simplistically in order for understanding to filter through to your mind. And do not be afraid or have any fear when the time comes for your spirit to return to the homeland. We would like to think we have evoked enough interest for the reader to explore further.

We have spoken on how you can learn how to blend with spirit's energies. Not only for communication purposes, but for the help and comfort that can be gained by knowing that our energies are there to help and guide you. We are your friends, we do not judge, our purpose is to give continuous love and support.

Spirit is indestructible. It lives on continuously. When you are on the earth in a physical body it is easy to forget that you are spirit in human form. When that spirit was in our world the main thoughts were of love, peace and forgiveness. Hate, greed and power did not exist; these thoughts are harboured on your earth.

Learn to forgive those who have treated you badly, spread love and happiness over hate, treat people kindly, protect and care for the animals of your world. These are precious beings that need respect just as much as the people of your earth do. Look after the environment where you reside. Your earth is a beautiful and wonderful place that should be given the respect it deserves. Love is the most powerful of emotions, it conquers all, let it spread throughout your world.

Finally, a farewell from us:

We cannot thank you enough. We hope you've found these conversations with spirit stimulating. You have spirit inside you, the God particle. Running your life at one hundred miles per hour, striving to make ends meet, climbing the career ladder or running a family is incredibly demanding. Never forget that you are loved. Never forget that you must look after yourself and make time to connect with spirit.

You are a messenger of spirit on earth. If you see someone who is losing hope or who has been weakened by circumstance, a kind word, a smile, a helping hand shines your light. Words can only do so much. Visit a spiritual church or arrange a reading from a spiritual medium to get personal proof, to witness evidence first hand. Your spiritual self may take time to surface. It will.

Treasure yourself. Look for the God particle in others. Care for Mother Earth.

Love to you from both sides of life.

Janet, Steve & Spirit

www.beingspirit.uk
spirit@beingspirit.uk

Appendix 1

About the Authors

Janet Neville. Wife, Mother, Spiritual Medium, Spiritual Messenger.

You met Janet keeping an audience enraptured. It was not always like that. For years she had zero idea of what was to come. She used to think you either had it or you didn't. Psychic ability that is, how wrong she was.

Janet's spiritual path began over twenty three years ago. In the beginning, all she felt was a low-level nagging feeling that something was missing. There was not a single sign of any psychic ability. It took an unexpected meeting with a medium to rock her back on her heels. She expected a reading (by the way, the words: reading and message are interchangeable in the context of spiritual communication) that would involve someone she knew who'd passed to the other side of life. Instead it was deeply spiritual.

She was told she would visit a spiritual church and sit in a circle to develop her gift.

What gift? She thought. A few days later she found herself in Barnes Church. She didn't care for the prayers or hymns and wondered why on earth she had gone and couldn't get out quick enough. Something drew her back. It took months before she could settle down and relax. She was invited to join a circle, even though she didn't have a clue what a circle was. The magnet grew stronger.

Spirit works in different ways with different people. The first few months were spent with Janet getting familiar with their energies and increasingly feeling their presence. In time and with dedication spirit began to channel messages through Janet. Her spirit guides have stressed that it is they who instigate the session and it is them who want to make contact to someone regardless of the belief system they follow. Often the message that someone is happy and safe in spirit is the reassurance people seek. Spirit is a universal presence for everyone. If you'd like to witness a demonstration of spiritual Mediumship like the one Janet gave, enter Spiritual Churches into your search engine and go along. You'll be warmly welcomed.

Today, Janet continues her channelling work at spiritual church services and gives private readings. In addition to describing someone in spirit to their loved ones by their physical appearance, Janet also provides details of their personality and mannerisms to reinforce the evidence, to prove their loved ones are still with them in spirit.

Steve Bridger: Writer and once a sceptic.

The day I entered a spiritualist church I was in a negative, sceptical frame of mind. Three little letters after the word 'spiritual' put me on high alert, three letters that changed the word from spiritual to spiritualism. I was totally okay with things spiritual but the words spiritualist and spiritualism suggested a strange movement I knew little about.

Plucking up courage, I reached for the door handle and stepped inside. There was no altar just a simple raised platform. A copy of Holman Hunt's painting of *'The Light of the World'* and a list of hymns beginning with *'Morning has Broken'* hung on the back wall. Smiling faces greeted me with a cheery welcome.

As a child if I had questions about the Bible or religion the response was always the same: have faith, accept the word of God; believe.

As a child I wanted more. As an adult I wanted hard evidence. Was I about to get it?

I stepped through the door on that particular day because I was doing some research on a short story with a spiritual theme. Also, I was silently grieving from a recent loss. For a small fee you could opt for either a fifteen or thirty minute session with a medium. Willing only to invest a small amount to confirm this would be a complete waste of time, I opted for the short session. Sure enough I was right. After fifteen minutes the medium had nothing to tell me, nada. There was an uncomfortable moment as we both shifted in our seats. The medium asked for more time, she could see I was unimpressed. She sat down again.

In the nineteenth minute she began to speak, her voice slower and deeper. She described the passing of my best friend. I knew what happened in general, but the accuracy, the detail, of her message was astounding. The vivid description of his passing was the first part of the message. The second was for me to ask his close friends not to be angry with him. It was a misguided act of love.

Seventeen years have passed since that first message. During that time I've had messages from my father, grandmother and grandfather and Eddie Quinn the bass player in the band I worked with; along with repeated evidence from my best friend.

It was seventeen years before spirit judged the time was right for me to meet Janet and for us to write this book.

Appendix 2

Being Spirit Book Two
Life & the Afterlife: Our Parallel Worlds

Earth Side

Earth side will focus upon our human relationship with spirit. Spirit will provide more answers to questions that are uppermost in many minds. We'll provide detailed insights from spirit on their influence on our daily lives as spirits in human form.

Spirit Side

Spirit wants us to understand about their world of peace and love. We'll learn what it's like to exist in a state of pure energy and consciousness after we leave the material world. You already know that the physical world ends. Being Spirit Book Two aims to take away the fear of the unknown and understand that the spiritual world is endless.

Our Parallel Worlds are One

www.beingspirit.uk
spirit@beingspirit.uk